# a Very Vintage
# CHRISTMAS

# a Very Vintage CHRISTMAS

HOLIDAY COLLECTING, DECORATING *and* CELEBRATING

## BOB RICHTER

WITH PHOTOGRAPHY BY ETHAN DAVID KENT
FOREWORD BY CHRISTOPHER RADKO

Globe
Pequot

Guilford, Connecticut

TO EVERYONE WHO LOVES CHRISTMAS—
and to all those who passed that love onto us.
For me, they include Mom, Dad, Nana, Grandma,
Robin, Johnny, Walter, Sharon, and Clint.

## Globe Pequot

An imprint of Rowman & Littlefield

Distributed by NATIONAL BOOK NETWORK

Copyright © 2016 by Bob Richter

PHOTOGRAPHY BY **Ethan David Kent**
ADDITIONAL PHOTOS: vii © Christopher Radko; xii, 22, 23, 106
© Bob Richter; 2, 4, 98 © Library of Congress; 3, 85, 102–103,
104, 105, 108, 151, 157, 161, 164, 166 © Thinkstock; 20, 55,
57, 101, 113 Licensed by Shutterstock.com; 24, 27 © Daniel
Yund; 107, 109 © Carrie Sansing; 181 © Blake Drummond.

British Library Cataloguing in Publication
Information Available

Library of Congress Cataloging-in-Publication
Data Available

ISBN 978-1-4930-2214-4
978-1-4930-2213-7 (e-book)

∞™  The paper used in this publication
meets the minimum requirements
of American National Standard for
Information Sciences—Permanence of
Paper for Printed Library Materials,
ANSI/NISO Z39.48-1992.

DESIGN BY **Karla Baker**

# TABLE of CONTENTS

vii    FOREWORD Christopher Radko

xi    Introduction

1    CHAPTER 1
**Christmas Decorating History**

21    CHAPTER 2
**Finding Vintage Christmas**

37    CHAPTER 3
**Ornaments**

81    CHAPTER 4
**Lights**

99    CHAPTER 5
**Outdoor Décor**

111    CHAPTER 6
**Putting It All Together**

145    CHAPTER 7
**No Tree? No Problem.**

165    CHAPTER 8
**Give a Vintage Gift**

177    CHAPTER 9
**Cards, Wrapping, Tags, and Other Ephemera**

191    CHAPTER 10
**Entertaining the Vintage Way**

199    CHAPTER 11
**Storing and Preserving Your Vintage Holiday Finds**

205    **In Conclusion**

207    **Appendix**

207    **A List of the Top US Flea Markets at Which to Find Vintage Christmas Items**

208    **Index**

209    **About the Photographer**

210    **About the Author**

# FOREWORD

I've always loved Christmastime—the shimmering tinsel and twinkling lights, the age-old carols and festive parties. All of it. But for me, Christmas isn't just one solitary day. Paraphrasing Charles Dickens, I make a point of "keeping the spirit of Christmas in my heart" all year long. This spirit of connection informs my day-to-day choices, and strengthens my journey. My choice to keep a bit of Christmas connectivity alive every day may seem dreamy and poetic to some, but I've found that it's got practical real life applications too—with all the fun that goes with it.

   "But how do I do this?," you may be asking. "Where do I begin?" A way that works for me is by understanding how vintage objects, especially holiday decorations, can serve as vehicles of connectivity. Existing outside the time in which they were first made and used, they can now inspire and connect people today. *This is what Bob Richter does.* And I can tell you, Bob doesn't just LOVE Christmas, he LIVES it!! This mirthful book shows us how Bob makes magic with vintage Christmas, and it's a joy to read. Bob connects the past with the present, and breathes life into the whole picture—something I realize that I've also been doing since I was a kid. And if you are reading this right now, I'll bet it's something you'll find worthwhile doing too!

   Bob engagingly writes about his adventures in flea markets and antiquing world over. For Bob, flea markets are like giant movable department stores. He adds that dealers naturally love art and history, and will enthusiastically share their knowledge with you. To the curious at heart, learning about the who, what, when, where, and how of your purchases opens up unimaginable new vistas to stories of forgotten

## BOB DOESN'T JUST
### LOVE CHRISTMAS,
#### HE LIVES IT!!

Behind this photo of the author and his grandmother is a now-vintage holly ball ornament by Christopher Radko.

craftsmanship, faraway places and long-past times. What a great way to learn more about our world.

Bob's discovered that you can take anything old, and make it new and relevant to your life again. To me, that widens the playing field. We don't have to rely just on what's cookie cutter new at the big box mall. Not when there's a world of lost beauty ready to be reclaimed. Shopping flea markets is the ultimate "green" endeavor, plus it means shopping local, both support the community. Flea market treasures can turn a bland house into a signature expression of personal taste. It's a way letting your heart take form.

I see each vintage ornament and antique trim as a time machine, containing within it the joy of so many people and Christmases of yore, all leading up to today. Their long ago celebrations, the spirit of Christmas past, inform each new holiday. By incorporating vintage holiday decorations into today's holidays, we are bringing deeper meaning to the way we keep these special days. Vintage objects reconnect us with our own past. Remember that little cotton ball snowman you made in third grade? I sure do!

Many of you know the story of my 12-foot family Christmas tree toppling over, sending hundreds of delicate glass ornaments crashing to the floor. Seeing the devastation before her, my grandmother promptly informed me that I had "ruined Christmas forever!" Yikes!! I had no idea then that I'd somehow one day turn this holiday catastrophe into an ornament empire. All I knew is that for the moment, I too felt shattered. But, I also understood the connection and the loss each family member felt. Growing up, I remember hearing things like, "Oh, look, this is the ornament we got when we were married," which my mom would tell my dad, while attaching an ornament hook to a winsome glass snowman. Once all the colored lights were hung on the branches, my granddad would say, "This ornament belonged to your great grandmother," as he handed me a tiny Santa with a green chenille tree. He would suggest, "Place it in the center of the tree, for everyone to see." When I was sitting on the couch with my Aunt Francis, admiring the finished tree, she would often remind me, "There's that unicorn ornament we got when you were first born, Christopher." And then she'd give me a hug.

True enough, there is a story behind each ornament. For most families, the Christmas tree is a family diary. Lighted from within, and resplendent with sparkle, the tree is an annual gathering place. It's a focal point for connection between events and people. The journey of each decoration is the voyage of our own legacy. Ornaments, and actually *all* our holiday decorations, are memory makers, connecting us to the people and the moments of our lives

After my family tree crashed, I began searching for vintage and antique decorations to regain some of that seemingly lost magic. What I found was oh so much more!

I have come to appreciate that when we decorate our homes, we create a heightened experience of these holidays not just for ourselves, but for others too. It's one of the reasons we often place our tree by the front window of our living room, so its beauty can be enjoyed by passersby, people we may never actually meet, but still recognize in our shared humanity.

We are literally highlighting these days, with shared experiences and gatherings, and saying, "Hey, there's more to life than just the daily grind. Let's get together and celebrate life!" For me, through the warm memories they evoke, ornaments and decorations bring a smile to our faces, lift our spirits, and connect us with each other. How amazing is that? These are tangible objects that contain an intangible essence, maybe it's *love*?

Going vintage is a way of including a wider world in your home. As songwriter Peter Allen wrote, "You can go backwards, when forward fails . . . because everything old is new again." It's definitely not about living in the past, or being sad in an exaggerated and self-indulgent way, which perhaps some people associate with sentimentality. Instead, as Bob points out, it's a highly creative and personal way of affectionately embracing our legacies, while at the same time, enhancing the fullness of our present world. In this way, sentimentality is beneficial and life giving. It's a sign that you are feeling with your heart. And with your heart, the creative possibilities are endless.

I invite you to breathe new life into your own family's decorations, and blend them with sparkly flea market finds from the past. Let this book be your passport to new adventures in life. You'll be enriching your home, and your heart, this Christmas!

—CHRISTOPHER RADKO

# Introduction

## "I WILL HONOUR CHRISTMAS IN MY HEART, AND TRY TO KEEP IT ALL THE YEAR."
### – Charles Dickens

It's often been said that Christmas is for children. Most of the yuletide propaganda and advertising serve to support that theory. When was the last time you saw an image of Santa with a bag full of presents for adults? I would be quick to point out, however, that children seem to need Christmas least of all, since the fortunate majority of them maintain an innocence, joy, and hopefulness that so many people lose as they grow older.

At Christmastime, however, our inner child has a chance to awaken—and to not be judged for embodying all of the things the years often take away. What's better than decorating a tree? Shopping for presents for loved ones? Singing Christmas carols? Few things, as far as I'm concerned. Sometimes these activities, when shared with loved ones, help us to exercise emotional muscles like joy and wonder that kids get to exercise every day.

So maybe instead of saying that Christmas is for children, we can say that Christmas is for the child in all of us. Christmas is the time when he or she can come out to play, and to enjoy the many gifts that are all around us.

### May the true spirit of CHRISTMAS dwell in your heart all year long.

Bob at age four with a tree decorated as a surprise from his brother, Johnny.

*A Very Vintage Christmas* embodies the nostalgia and sentimentality associated with the holiday season. Vintage ornaments, lights, decorations, cards, and wrapping all conjure up happy memories of Christmases past and serve as tangible mementos of holidays shared with family and friends. In fact, finding these objects, decorating with them, and sharing them with others brings an instant feeling of comfort and joy. *A Very Vintage Christmas* is open to all and completely scalable based on budget, taste, interest level, and level of imagination.

*A Very Vintage Christmas* grew out of my own passion for collecting holiday décor. My collection grows each year, but the basic foundation was laid when I was a young boy. My dad would take me to auctions and one day when I climbed in his pickup truck, he handed me a box of beautiful ornaments, including a blue jay, a Santa Claus, some bells, ice cream cones, and other special figures. "It's time you started collecting something," he said, ". . . and I know you like Christmas."

So collect I did—and still do. That original box has grown into a collection that hovers at around 2,500 and counting. Each year I have an 8-foot evergreen in my living room, and I see lots of those ornaments my dad gave me over three decades ago.

Still even earlier in my childhood, I recall a December afternoon when my mom brought me home from the pediatrician only to find my big brother had put up a tree for me of my very own in my room. It was decorated with lights and ornaments that were new at the time, but are now vintage. I have such a powerfully happy memory of coming home and finding that tree and that same feeling of wonder still comes over me each year at the holidays. And like many with great memories of childhood Christmases, I still keep my eyes open at flea markets and other venues for ornaments like my brother used to decorate that very special tree.

As my grandmother grew older, she took pleasure in letting me decorate her tree, and I have many happy memories of doing it. Now one of my favorite and most treasured ornaments is her favorite Santa Claus. Each year when I hang him on my tree, I think of her and smile. And that's just a glimpse into the wonderful sentimentality that I fully embrace about the holidays.

Choirboy candles from Bob's grandmother.

Like many kids, I also made ornaments, and even had a whole tree decorated with ones I created with my own two hands (and my mom's help). There's one that I keep out all year. It says "May the true spirit of Christmas dwell in your heart all year long." As a child, I wanted Christmas to go beyond December 25. And it sure did—and still does. I collect Christmas all year long, and have been known to watch *It's A Wonderful Life* in July. And I know I'm not alone . . .

Like me, many begin their collecting by expanding on a box of family ornaments, or some go out looking for the kind of ornaments their families had, but have long ago discarded. My hope is that this book will help everyday collectors and enthusiasts to build their own collection and discover how to make the most of what they've got.

No matter the scale on which you decorate or gift give or sing carols, I encourage you to let your inner child enjoy the wonder of it all. And from my home to yours, I wish you a Very Vintage Christmas!

—BOB RICHTER

# Christmas Decorating History

With the saturation of Christmas ornaments, lights, and décor on the market, it's hard to believe that just 100 years ago *only one in five American households had a tree* at the holidays. And 25 years before that, they were pretty much concentrated in Europe.

What began as a Pagan ritual and was later adopted by Christians in Germany in the 1600s, decorating a Christmas tree has come a long way. While there are some reports of Christmas trees in America as early as the 1700s, tree decorating really flourished in the US at the turn of the century. Today most households that observe Christmas in this country have a tree. It has evolved from a religious expression to a celebration of a season and of peace, comfort, joy, and abundance.

While the very first Christmas tree farm in the US emerged in 1901 in Trenton, New Jersey, most Americans headed to their local forest (or backyard!) and chopped down their own trees until the 1940s and 1950s. For many finding the tree and bringing it home (whether in the forest or on a farm) became a tradition and marked the beginning of the Christmas festivities. And it still does!

Early trees were decorated with candles and paper ornaments, which proved to be beautiful, yet dangerous. So when Thomas Edison developed the first string of electric Christmas lights in 1880 (only one year after he created the standard light bulb), Christmas trees were on their way to becoming safer and more hearty.

Since Edison's early strings needed their own generator, they were reserved for the One Percent, costing about $2,000 to get up and running. The White House trail blazed in 1895 as President Grover Cleveland ordered its first electrically lit tree, which featured over 100 colored lights.

Still candles remained on most American trees until the price began to drop (and more households were wired for electricity) in the 1930s. Candles were typically placed in metal holders that clipped onto the branches of trees. Lighting happened as part of a ritual on Christmas Eve or Christmas Day and candles were often swiftly blown out for safety and efficiency. This magic glow, however short it was to take place, came to symbolize the warmth and spirit of the holiday season.

Early decorations in America fell into two categories: 1) Homemade—strings of popcorn, construction paper cutouts, etc. and 2) Store-bought—mercury glass ornaments and elaborate die-cut paper ornaments embellished with tinsel and glitter imported from Europe—mostly Germany.

In 1880, Woolworth's began stocking German blown-glass ornaments and sales dramatically escalated on a yearly basis as a multimillion dollar industry was born. Germany had a monopoly on importing ornaments to the US until the mid-1920s when other countries hopped on the bandwagon. One of their first import

Store displays of toys in 1941/42.

rivals was Japan, who quickly established a formidable presence in the market.

Ornaments also came to America with immigrants who brought them along with their own customs and traditions. While Germany is credited with the development of traditional blown-glass ornaments, many other European countries like Poland, The Czech Republic, and Italy each had their own take on décor.

Since store-bought ornaments were also more expensive and considered a luxury, homemade ornaments were quite common. Children often made them in school or at home with their parents. Fruits, nuts, and berries also routinely adorned trees.

A 1950s living room at Christmas.

Decorating the tree was typically reserved for Christmas Eve, and in most homes, children were barred from the room. It was also quite common for children to be told that Santa Claus came and decorated the tree while they slept on Christmas Eve. In the morning, they'd wake not only to a fully decorated tree, but presents as well. Imagine the work for parents! But from the stories I hear of those who had this tradition, it was pure magic, and kept an innocence and wonder about the holiday alive and kicking.

For many, Christmas trees arrived just in time to bring a glimmer of cheer to one of the darkest periods in US history: The Great Depression. While funds were restricted for most, a tree could be generally cut down for free and decorated with ornaments made from odds and ends already around the home. As a symbol of hope and faith, it seemed the Christmas tree was now more important than ever.

Of course everyone knows about the enormous tree decorated each year in New York City at Rockefeller Center. But few know of the humble beginnings of that now world-famous tree. On Christmas Eve 1931, the workers (in a display of gratitude for the work they had during this harrowing time) erected

Washington, D.C. Christmas shopping in Woolworth's five and ten cent store, 1941.

the first tree at the site of Rockefeller Center. Decorated with paper garlands, strings of cranberries, and even tin cans, the first tree there was indeed a symbol of hope and the prosperity that was to come in the years ahead.

By the late 1930s, America hopped on the ornament creation bandwagon as Max Eckhardt & Sons introduced a line of machine-made ornaments sold under the name "Shiny Brite." A German immigrant, Eckhardt knew silvered glass ornaments well, and he took his knowledge, married it with innovation, and created an empire. And his timing could not have been more perfect, as WWII loomed on the horizon. Americans wanted to buy American-made ornaments, so a multimillion-dollar American industry was born. To ensure shoppers knew these were American ornaments, an image of Uncle Sam shaking hands with Santa Claus was on the front of Shiny Brite boxes. Patriotism and Christmas were formally introduced, and during the following years, they were inseparable.

Shiny Brite also tapped into popular assembly line production technology that created ornaments in lightning speed. In fact they reportedly produced roughly 2,000 ornaments a minute by harnessing the same technology that was used to make light bulbs. This was also where the name "Shiny Brite" was born, since the factories also produced the shiny bulbs used to bring light into homes.

Eckhardt initially tapped The Corning Glass company in Corning, New York, to make the ornaments, which were then painted in New Jersey and Long Island and then in other locations as demand grew.

For years, many referred to Christmas balls as "bulbs," and this American innovation with its light bulb roots, is where that name likely originated.

As the US joined the Allied Forces and WWII was well underway, rationing changed the face of American ornaments. Silvered glass ornaments were now replaced with simple, non-reflective painted glass, and their formerly metal caps were replaced with paper ones.

As patriotism hit an all-time high, the American Christmas tree became a symbol of much more than Christmas: It represented unity, fortitude, and courage. Many patriotic ornaments (red, white, and blue balls and bells) were also produced during this time. Today ornaments made during those years are highly prized by collectors (myself included!).

Often times, in a box of older ornaments, string will be added to each one as a hanger. This is also often representative of wartime conservancy. Each time I come across such ornaments I'm reminded of how everyone did their part, from small to large efforts during the war years.

After WWII ended, ornaments reflected the post-war optimism that was widespread in the US. The silver and metal returned and brightly colored balls of various shapes and sizes where produced by many companies.

Technology advancements, many of which came about as a result of the war effort, also added to tree decorating becoming an easier task. Lights, for instance, used to be headache for many a family, since when one bulb burned out, the whole string stopped working.

In the 1950s ornaments took on the look of the Atomic Age with shapes that resembled spaceships, planets, and stars. Plastics also emerged on the scene as a viable, widespread 'unbreakable' alternative to glass ornaments. Lights, too, were now offered in various colors and sizes. An immensely popular variety known as "bubble lights" (first introduced in 1946) rapidly grew in popularity and the electric glow of Christmas took on a whole new look.

The first recorded use of outdoor lights was in San Diego in 1904 and then they made an appearance in New York City in 1912. By the 1920s General Electric even sponsored community lighting contests. But until post–WII, outdoor lights were not in the picture for many homes. By the 1950s the popularity of outdoor lighting was in full swing. Now average American homes could have not only a lit Christmas tree inside, but an illuminated tree (or trees), roof, and lawn on the outside. As efforts to "keep up with the Jones" mounted, entire neighborhoods began to give off a Yuletide glow.

By this time in history Christmas décor had become less cost prohibitive. Ornaments, lights, and decorations were widely available and many have fond memories of shopping for them at department stores, and certainly Woolworths and other five and dimes.

If I could be catapulted back into history I would love to be dropped down in post-war America at a Woolworths store during the holiday season. I've seen many black and white images of holiday shoppers buying ornaments and other décor, and I study these images like an archeologist. Those items are the very same ones I see out today when I'm hunting for vintage holiday treasures.

By the 1960s, Americans had choices when it came to buying real or artificial trees. It was at this time that in addition to traditional green, the first silver trees were manufactured. Silver trees became immensely popular and their accompanying rotating color wheels transformed them into glowing red, yellow, green, and blue ultra-modern décor. Trees during this period also took on a more minimalist quality. The color wheels replaced lights on a tree, and ornaments were often simple balls. This new style wasn't for everyone, but those who embraced it often had Midcentury Modern décor, which lent itself to a space age tree.

In 1965, CBS first aired *A Charlie Brown Christmas*, and it became an instant holiday classic and has aired every year since. In it, Charlie Brown searches for the true meaning of Christmas and begins to feel bogged down by the growing commercialism of Christmas. In many ways a social commentary about what Christmas was becoming, it finds poor Charlie Brown downtrodden, with a pitiful branch of a tree.

That branch comes to life as he and his friends each bring a bit of themselves to the decorating and give it a little love. For many, the special is deeply sentimental and embodies the true spirit of Christmas. What it also inadvertently did, was give everyone permission to have a tree that wasn't perfect, enormous or lavishly decorated!

The 1970s saw a return to tradition, with handmade ornaments making a big comeback (think *Little House on the Prairie*) and European glass ornaments again becoming widely available. Companies like Hallmark also began to create collectible ornaments that became hugely popular and remain widely collected today.

Hallmark's "Keepsake Ornaments," first introduced in 1973, incentivized parents to begin building collections for their children so they could enjoy them and have them for their own home when they grew up. This tradition caught on and continues to this day. I know many people whose parents bought them a Keepsake Ornament each year through adulthood. When they moved into their own homes, their parents would often give them their own collection, which had been accumulated over the years.

On the other end of the spectrum, some embraced the disco craze that hit the country, adorning their trees with items that took their cues from *Saturday Night Fever*, from satin ornaments to disco balls. These ornaments became wildly popular and then, just as disco did, fell out of vogue. Since their popularity peaked and waned in a short time span, these are likely to be a hot area of Christmas collecting, as everything comes around again.

Many 1970s ornaments were imported from Japan, Taiwan, and Hong Kong. Popular themes were cartoon characters such as the Peanuts, the Flintstones, and Loony Tunes. By the late 1970s department stores also started creating "theme trees" to market decorations by color, style, and subject.

In the 1980s, Christopher Radko emerged on the scene, introducing decorations made in the style of vintage ones, and an array of his own new designs. This was a time when fine blown-glass ornaments were falling by the wayside, being replaced by less fragile plastic and Styrofoam decor. Reviving and often even improving upon nineteenth-century glass-blowing techniques, his joyful and detailed ornaments were first made in Poland in 1985.

He then expanded his body of work in Germany, Czech Republic, and Italy, highlighting the artisan traditions of local craftsmen. Each country had willing glassblowers who were up to the challenge of creating more elaborate ornaments. They also had caches of antique examples and molds (many not used in decades) that Radko revived—and in many cases uplifted in detail and quality. His creations were not being sold at the five and dime store as the antique ones were, but at upper tier department stores and gift and specialty shops.

Radko even began producing new ornaments made in the vintage American style, harnessing the famous Shiny Brite name and the nostalgic mid-twentieth-century feel he grew up with. Widely collected and treasured, Radko's ornaments remain very popular to this day.

By the end of the twentieth century into today, there are ornaments, lights, and decorations for every taste and budget. Vintage ornaments from all of the decades can be found at flea markets, auctions, and estate sales. People's individual collections become highly sentimental and are routinely passed down from generation to generation

Each year as the ornaments are unpacked, a floodgate of memories is typically unpacked along with them. "Baby's First Christmas," hand-made ornaments from childhood art classes, ornaments from a couple's first tree, souvenirs from travels—the list goes on and on. Pieces like this have emotional value that far outweighs anything in the financial realm.

In fact, it seems that along the lines of emotional value, boxes of ornaments and other decorations in a home can be right up there among a family's most prized possessions. Many trees are like scrapbooks for families, with various styles and ornaments from many decades, both homemade and store bought. In fact, for many, the tree is a likened to their family tree, with ornaments that belonged to grandparents, ones that were gifted by other relatives, and ones that were bought that very year.

Of course it you aren't fortunate enough to have such boxes of memories, it's never too late to start. Ornaments like those that were on your childhood tree, your parent's tree, and your grandparent's tree are out there, and when they are found, can feel just as precious as the originals. Great places to look are flea markets, tag sales, auctions, and antiques shops. For more about that, head over to Chapter Two.

For those of us who are super crazy for Christmas, there is usually more than one tree, and no room of the house goes undecorated. Themed trees and trees decorated by color or era are also becoming more and more common. But whether a house has one tree or ten trees—or a tree made up of family heirloom ornaments or brand new décor, what matters is the sentiment behind it all. The truth is (for me anyway), that a house with a Christmas tree, just feels like home.

Coca Cola did their part to carve out the ideal image of Santa Claus. Beginning in the early 1930s, Coke would have a very special, idealized Santa image each year to advertise their product. Designed by Haddon Sundblom, this store display poster shows elves waiting on Santa by hand and foot. As they serve him his turkey dinner, they also pour him a tall glass of Coke.

*Faith is believing when common sense tells you not to.*

—FRED GAILY,
MIRACLE ON 34th STREET

THEY REMEMBERED ME!

Norman Rockwell's contribution to our culture and visual consciousness is a great one. He created so many iconic holiday images. This is one of my personal favorites. It depicts a WWI soldier receiving a package of gifts from home. The print is from 1917 and is titled "They Remembered Me!"

At last it is Christmas Eve, frosty and smelling of snow.

Peter stops at Mary's house for cocoa and ginger-bread. Then he goes home to hang up his stocking. Mary hangs hers by the fireplace.

In the morning, Peter races over to show Mary his striped necktie and his cigar—of chocolate. Mary gives Peter his fire engine. And he gives her a tiny bed for her new doll. They are both very pleased. Peter and Mary play under the tree all morning.

The perfect Christmas scene is depicted in this *Little Golden Book*. The mantle is adorned, the nativity set is arranged, the tree is trimmed, and the toys are laid out.

This 1930s book detailing customs and stories of Christmas in other countries also includes carols and other items of interest.

This 1926 literary magazine called *The Golden Book* showcases frame-worthy cover art depicting a flapper (note the short haircut) lighting candles on a stylized tree. Contents include short stories by top authors of the day.

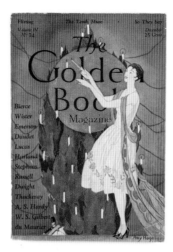

In the early and mid-twentieth century many people belonged to fraternal orders like The Elks Club (my grandfather was a member). Some even had their own publications. This December 1941 issue of *The Elks Magazine* is pretty stunning, as it depicts a very glam gal lighting the candles on a tree.

The 1920s ushered in a new crop of highbrow literary and fashion magazines like *Judge*. This particular "Christmas Number" is just plain gorgeous.

This 1944 issue of *Esquire* depicts Lady Liberty showing a little leg as Santa brings fellas home from the war. The articles and cartoons feature a veritable who's who of luminaries at the time. In the lower left corner it also encourages reader to invest in War Bonds.

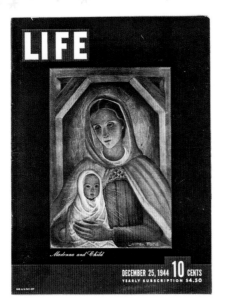

The Christmas 1944 issue of *Life* magazine features a painting of The Madonna and Child by Lauren Ford. It was the only color cover of the magazine during WWII.

The Interwoven Sock Company makes no bones about who the enemies are in this 1944 ad, which appeared in *Esquire* magazine. Santa takes on bad guys as the Allied troops are one more mighty step closer to victory.

"Home, Home At Last" was the tagline of this ad for Kevinator appliances, which appeared in the December 25, 1944, issue of *Life* magazine. It's photo and copy suggests a time in the not-too-distant future when families would be reunited and could begin to plan for the future.

Norman Rockwell's iconic cover of the December 23, 1944, issue of *The Saturday Evening Post* is titled "Union Train Station, Chicago, Christmas." It depicts the bustle of holiday travelers, shoppers, and servicemen and has become a classic holiday image.

A quintessential Christmas cover of *Better Homes & Gardens* magazine from 1933.

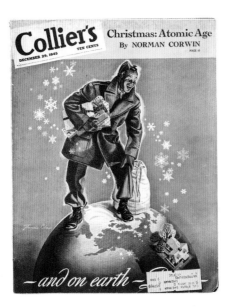

On the December 29, 1945, issue of *Collier's* magazine, a soldier is depicted, arms filled with presents, as he looks down on the home where he'll soon return.

In the earlier part of the twentieth century, immigrants in the US often wanted publications from their homeland, written in their native language and depicting their customs. This 1927 Christmas issue of Sweden's *Husmodern* magazine is a great example of this.

The years following WWII saw families once again shopping at full speed for Christmas. This cover of the December 1947 issue of *Better Homes and Gardens* shows children gathered around a department store Santa Claus. It was this same year that *Miracle on 34th Street*—a movie all about a magical department store Santa—was released in theaters.

The 1953 issue of *Arizona Highways* magazine suggested a Southwest take on Christmas. As more Americans moved to wide open spaces, publications like this rose up to greet them.

A late 1800s German Christmas book (bottom left) tells the story of the Weihnachtman, who was the fellow who became our Santa Claus. In this story, told with beautiful color and graphics, the man in the red cloak has angel helpers who decorate the tree and leave gifts for good girls and boys.

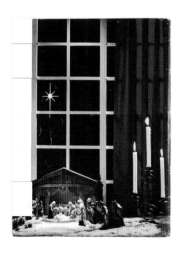

This 1950s Howard Gale Santa is definitely one jolly fellow. Many people recall having this particular Santa in their homes at Christmastime. He's got a red velvet suit trimmed with white faux fur and a papier-mâché face with great expression. This particular Santa also came in pink and white.

This early 1900s German clip on Weihnachtsman was in that first box of ornaments from my dad. Many such early 1900s ornaments were brought to the US by immigrants, while others were purchased here at Woolworth's and other retailers that began selling ornaments.

Santa and his reindeer took on many looks over the years. This 1930s version is on wheels, so it could double as a toy. Santa's sleigh, adorned with stars, also has space to hold candy or small gifts.

A standing composition Santa and a seated metal Santa in his sleigh . . . these 1930s figures were inexpensive and easy to display just about anywhere. Now they are easily found at flea markets.

A bisque German Father Christmas figure, this version shows how the earlier European versions of St. Nick were significantly more slender than the fellow we know today.

The Weinachtman and his angel sidekick have worked their magic, and these good little German children are rewarded with a perfect Christmas tree (note the candles) and an array of toys.

# CHAPTER 2

# Finding Vintage Christmas

**A**s I mentioned earlier, my hunt for vintage Christmas began when my father gave me a box of ornaments and suggested I begin collecting. In this chapter I'll outline many places where vintage holiday gems can be found. I've done all of these things, but one way I stumbled on a real treasure trove; I'll share right off the bat. When I was about ten and my collection was rapidly growing, it dawned on me to put an ad in the local newspaper. I was very clear about what I wanted—and I got it!

One day I received a call from a lovely older woman who read the ad and said she had vintage Christmas in her home and would be happy for me to come by and take a look. My Dad drove me there and after we entered, she brought in some old boxes filled with wonderful ornaments, lights, and decorations. I made an offer on the spot, and purchased them all. I suppose you may call this whole scenario precocious, but I share it to underscore the fact that where there's a will, there's a way.

To this day many of the things I purchased on that afternoon are still in my collection, and frankly, they are still some of my favorites. However you find your vintage holiday treasures, enjoy the journey, and don't be afraid to be creative!

## MAKE FLEA MARKETS YOUR FIRST STOP

Flea marketing in New York City.

Flea markets are my main hunting grounds. I like to say that if you want to understand a place and the people who live there, go to the local flea market. It's really a sociological and historical representation of just about anywhere you can point on a map. One thing you can find at just about every flea market in the US is an assortment of vintage Christmas decorations, lights, and ephemera.

That said, I start my shopping early, since just like in retail stores, certain merchandise at these venues fluctuates in price depending upon the season. The truth is that Christmas items are often the last thing on someone's mind in the summer, so I take advantage of that fact and rake in the bargains.

In the summer months, this décor is literally a quarter of the price it will be in October to December, when dealers mark it up to for impulse shoppers who are in the holiday mood and on a mission.

In addition to the fantastic vintage finds at flea markets, you are likely to find a number of fantastic people who sell there. Once you begin to purchase Christmas items from them, they may turn out to be good friends, teachers, and even personal shoppers for you.

I've been fortunate to have this experience with many dealers who enjoy sharing their vintage Christmas finds with me, since they know I appreciate their work. Not everyone realizes how challenging work can be for flea market vendors. Many of them spend time digging through attics and basements at estate sales just to find a handful of special things to bring to a market. Since I can't get to as many estate sales as I would like, I count on these dealers to find me special things.

With many vendors I've become a repeat customer, so not only do they often give me great prices, they'll also give me first pick. In fact, I have one dealer and friend named Armand who keeps the vintage Christmas he finds under the table for me, so I get first pick. Friends like that don't come along every day, so I am very grateful.

Armand and many others have also helped me to not only build upon my collection, but learn more and more about vintage Christmas ornaments, lights, decorations, and customs. It's like the vendors are my teachers and the vintage finds are our books. And I try my best to pass that knowledge on to those who are interested.

Antiquing in Santa Fe, New Mexico.

## ANTIQUES SHOPS ARE ALWAYS A GOOD IDEA

Like flea markets, many antiques shops also carry vintage Christmas items all year long, so keep your eyes open and you're sure to find some great pieces to start or add to your collection. Antiques shops, however, are likely to charge more for vintage Christmas since owners or dealers who sell there have to cover a higher rent. That said, my off-season rule applies in these venues as well.

One really great thing about shopping antiques shops during the holiday season, however, is that they often do a sensational job at setting the vintage holiday mood. In fact, since so many antiques dealers are also wonderful curators and decorators, antiques shops are likely to give you lots of decorating ideas to incorporate into your own home. And while you're feeling in the holiday mood, you'll likely buy something that will be very special.

In a later chapter I'll discuss giving vintage gifts for Christmas, so while you're at the antiques shop make sure to bring along your list. I'd much rather spend money at antiques shops than at a mall!

## GET ONLINE

Nowadays everyone shops online. Whether it's shoes or groceries or baby furniture, it seems people do more shopping from their computers than they do in person. Why should hunting for vintage Christmas be any different? Well, truth be told I'll say here and now that I think when it comes to shopping for all things vintage, I always prefer an in-person shopping

Antiquing in Rhinebeck, New York.

experience, as I love to interact with things, learn more about them, and often discover items I didn't know I wanted.

That said, finding vintage Christmas online has never been easier. Just enter "vintage Christmas" into the search box on eBay, Etsy, or any number of online venues, and thousands and thousands of things will come up. Of course you can refine your searching by item (balls, decorations, lights, etc.) and in many cases even by the decade in which they were made. The results can be dizzying but you are likely to stumble upon a treasure trove of vintage goodies.

Just like with flea markets, if you buy repeatedly from certain vendors, they may give you better prices and alert you when they find new things. That old rule of thumb that 90 percent of business comes from 10 percent of your customers definitely holds true . . . and vendors know it. So it's a win-win scenario!

A word of caution, however: Since the Internet is always open, you may unleash your inner vintage Christmas beast. Since many of these sites are auction format, you may also get bidding fever and over-pay for some things. So proceed with caution and have fun.

More than any other venue, however, online shopping sites can help you learn about vintage Christmas items, train your eye, and make you smarter about what's available and what you want to add to your collection.

## SHOP LIKE A DEALER

If you want to go straight to the source, you can do what antiques dealers do and shop estate sales and auctions. Since most homes in the US had Christmas items in the attic, basement, or garage, it's safe to say that there are lots of ornaments and other items out there at these venues.

For those who've never been to an estate sale, it is a unique experience you'll not soon forget. The owners of the home have either downsized or passed away, so everything in the house is for sale. It can be voyeuristic and sociologically fascinating to enter into a home, open drawers and boxes and see what you find. It can also be cutthroat in terms of competition, so if you see something you like, grab it. The truth is, unless you are a dealer, you may not attend many of these because often there is a long line to get inside and the wait can be a real challenge.

Still there is nothing cooler than finding someone's entire vault of vintage Christmas and adopting it into your life. I've had a lot of fun doing it and the bottom line is that estate sale prices are the lowest in the vintage food chain (which is why dealers shop there). If it's Christmas you're after, make a bee-line to the attic or basement and hope for the best.

Auctions are also wonderful places to find vintage Christmas and I've had much success at them. The best ones are estate auctions, which, as the name connotes, often sell off the entire tangible remains of someone's home. The best way to buy Christmas at these venues is in something called a "box lot," where you pay one price for everything. Once auctioneers begin separating items, the prices go up. Of course, the downside is that you may wind up purchasing some things you don't want . . . but it's all part of the game.

## GOING ON VACATION? DON'T FORGET TO THINK CHRISTMAS

Many people buy Christmas ornaments on their vacations. I do this as well, but for me, it is vintage ornaments and décor that I'm after. Of course I frequent flea markets and antiques shops when I travel, so whether my trip is domestic or international, I'm always on the hunt.

A note about US travel: As much as I love the West Coast, the best vintage Christmas is found on the East Coast. Why? It's older, and it's the first place European immigrants settled, and brought with them their ornaments. (For a list of top recommended flea markets, see the appendix at the end of this book.)

As for Europe, Germany, Austria, Hungary, and Czech Republic have been the best places I've found vintage Christmas. These countries (along with Poland) produced the most and earliest Christmas décor, so it just stands to reason that the supply is greatest in these areas. These countries really also perfected the mercury glass ornament, which is the most common and luminescent kind you'll find.

My most recent favorite vintage Christmas vacation find, however, wasn't in any of the above countries, but in France. While France doesn't typically have as many ornaments, they certainly do have a long history of Christmas decorating. My favorite find there was at the Porte de Vanvres flea market in Paris. It is a large, framed photo of a little boy lighting his Christmas tree. It was only 5 Euros and it fit perfectly in the bottom of my suitcase.

## HOW MUCH DO VINTAGE ORNAMENTS, LIGHTS, AND DÉCOR COST?

While this book is by no means a tedious price guide (those are available and are highly recommended if you want to get very serious about collecting). That said, there are vintage holiday items for sale at every budget and sensibility.

In general the older and more detailed ornaments are, the higher price they command. A great way to start is by purchasing basic round mercury glass balls, whether they are striped, plain, or adorned with images. They were mass-produced and in plentiful supply. You can find a box of them for between $5 and $20. Sometimes you can find them for much less, but there's no need to pay more.

The exception to the rule when it comes to Christmas balls is the Kugel (the earliest form of ball). Hallmarked by its signature brass cap with a ring through it, Kugels were mostly German or French and can cost up to $100 a piece. (For more on Kugels see the following chapter, all about ornaments).

Figural ornaments are on the higher end of the price spectrum. Bells and pinecones tend to be the most accessible at about $3 apiece whereas some, like an early Santa Claus, can cost hundreds of dollars.

Lights are relatively inexpensive at between $5 and $10 a box, but like with ornaments, the older or more unique they are, the more expensive they'll be. For example, a set of older bubble lights can cost about $100 in the original box.

My best advice for those looking to start buying vintage Christmas would be start slowly and grow your collection over time. The more you shop, the more you learn—about what is available and what you like most. Most importantly, have fun!

This 1940s rubber Santa figure is as round as he is tall. With hand-painted details and a hand waving to boys and girls, this guy is a real treat. Most years he resides under my tree.

Putting kids to work is easier when their tools are made to look like this 1950s shovel. Smaller in scale and designed to be utilitarian, I now honor the decorative value of this piece and usually prop it in a corner of my home.

Liberté, égalité, fraternité . . . some clever person long ago channeled all these things, along with creativity to fabricate this wonderful French Snow Queen decoration. Her sleigh is made from an old box of Christmas light bulbs, and adorned with tinsel and angel hair. She waves the French flag and is led by a celluloid reindeer. This is one of my very favorite vintage finds . . . and truly a one-of-a-kind treasure.

---

It seems as vintage nativity sets were lost or broken over the years, the Jesus figures were almost always saved. I found all of these at flea markets. I nestled the large composition figure in a 1930s French Art Deco bowl.

---

Patriotism was at an all-time high in America during WWII. From what I can gather, Christmas underscored it even more. This license plate encouraging people to buy war bonds is a treasured flea market find.

This 1920s miniature "Gablonzer" Czech tabletop tree is made of wire and green paper. Similar to the German feather tree, it is adorned with small, intricate blown glass ornaments and resides in a green glass base. Tiny trees like this are hard to find in the US, but thanks to the Internet, they can easily be acquired from reputable dealers in the Czech Republic.

This reproduction of a German feather tree comes in a traditional wooden base. Unlike the original versions, which were made of goose feathers, this one is synthetic. Typically adorned with small glass balls, this one, with its variegated greens and red berries, is great looking without any additional bells and whistles.

A trio of pink mid-twentieth-century bottle-brush trees. In graduated sizes with silver balls, these are both mod and nostalgic. And they are sought after by collectors.

An uncommon pair of green bottle brush trees, one retains its original "Made in Japan" tag. Likely from a 5 and 10 Cent store these are adorned with small, red mercury glass balls.

Adorned with sequins and beads, this little tree was always a part of my grandmother's holiday display. She made it in the 1950s as part of an activity in one of her clubs. After using it for many years, she gave it to me when I was a boy. Now it is always part of my holiday displays.

This Japanese green foil umbrella tree is a rare and wonderful find. It folds like an umbrella for easy storage, and the mercury glass balls come off easily for a swift set up and takedown. Likely made in the 1950s, this tree would make an excellent complement to any Midcentury Modern décor.

Known as a bottlebrush tree, this variety cropped up at 5 & 10 Cent stores to offer an easy, artificial tabletop alternative to a large tree. From the early 1950s, this example was flocked with white "snow" and adored with small red balls and tinsel. Falling under the category of kitsch, this one goes in my bathroom every year.

Originally part of a crèche scene in a church, these large early-twentieth-century composition angels have hand-painted detail and are a true pair, as they face each other. Many years these two adorn my mantle.

Other than the baby Jesus, angel figures are the most likely survivors from vintage nativity sets. These three composition figures are all from Germany. I keep them out on display all year long.

This German "Heinrichsen" Messenger Angel can be hung on the tree or easily stands alone. I keep him out all year long next to my perpetual calendar.

"Unbreakable" plastic became increasingly popular for Christmas decorations in the 1940s and 1950s. This metallic angel from The Bradford Company is great displayed on its own, as an ornament on the tree, or even as the topper for a smaller tree.

As plastics became more popular in the 1940s, the "Crystal Pine" tree emerged on the scene. Easy to assemble, the tree is made from clear plastic, and small mercury glass balls adorn each branch. It was also small, easy, and inexpensive—all key selling points at the time. I found this one in its original box.

This little forest of 1950s Gurley Novelty Company trees are more examples of decorative candles that were never burned. Still retaining their color and sparkle, they are fun, inexpensive vintage finds.

This pair of "Blinking" Christmas trees each takes two C batteries and are completely charming. Sold by a dealer who stumbled on "new" old stock from a store in Pennsylvania, they are vintage items in brand-new condition.

The colors and glittery accents on this die-cut German Santa are wonderful. The decoration is also remarkably well preserved.

All of these plastic and celluloid reindeer originally led Santa and his sleigh. Now each stands well on its own, or when put together in groupings like these. Just about every home had a version of these, so they often open a floodgate of memories when people see them.

In the 1950s, 1960s, and 1970s, Santa's elves began to gain more popularity. The trumpeter (with his flower horn) entertains his reclining rubber friend. My mom had many of these in our home in the 1970s.

· ◆ ·‒‒‒‒‒‒‒‒‒‒‒‒‒‒‒‒‒‒‒‒‒‒‒‒‒‒‒‒‒‒‒‒‒· ◆ ·

This little rubber "hugger" elf was always on the side of my mom's wall-mount phone in the kitchen in our home at the holidays. Long before "Elf on the Shelf," these guys sat all over the house . . . and were often moved around to entertain children of all ages.

· ◆ ·‒‒‒‒‒‒‒‒‒‒‒‒‒‒‒‒‒‒‒‒‒‒‒‒‒‒‒‒‒‒‒‒‒· ◆ ·

Pinecone gnomes add a whimsical touch to any Christmas display. With plastic heads and felt adornments, their bodies are actual pinecones. These two were made in Japan in the 1950s.

# Ornaments

As a lifelong collector of vintage Christmas ornaments, I can confidently tell you that I'm not an expert. The same goes for me with antiques. The truth is, while I know a lot, I'm always learning and always discovering things I've never seen or heard of before.

While I decorate each year for my own pleasure, I also take great joy in sharing my trees with loved ones. It's fun to see people's reactions when they see vintage ornaments. Nearly everyone says something like "My grandmother had one of these" or "These remind me of my aunt," etc. etc.

Vintage ornaments add that nostalgic, sentimental vibe to a home, and people often have a very warm and fuzzy response to them.

I also love the information that vintage décor reveals about other times and other places. For example, WWII ornaments made in the US were un-silvered and often had paper caps, as all metal was needed for the war effort. Early German ornaments known as "kugels" were much heavier and had fancy brass tops. Czech ornaments were often made of glass beads. The list goes on and on.

## THE EARLIEST ORNAMENTS

When decorating for Christmas emerged, ornaments were simple and for the chosen few. Some of the earliest ornaments are German (and sometimes French) kugels, which are heavy balls with large brass caps. Many German immigrants brought them to the US, so they are available, but tend to be rather pricey.

Kugels were generally round balls that came in small, medium, and large sizes. There are also ribbed orbs and grape clusters. The most common colors are blue, green, red, silver, and gold.

The first kugels in my collection were a gift from a very kind pharmacist who worked with one of my best friends in high school. She told him of my love of vintage Christmas, and he gave me a box that included two large, heavy cobalt blue kugels and a few smaller gold and green ones. They quickly became the pride of my collection and are still on my trees to this day.

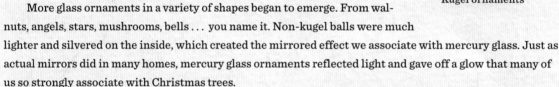

Kugel ornaments

More glass ornaments in a variety of shapes began to emerge. From walnuts, angels, stars, mushrooms, bells . . . you name it. Non-kugel balls were much lighter and silvered on the inside, which created the mirrored effect we associate with mercury glass. Just as actual mirrors did in many homes, mercury glass ornaments reflected light and gave off a glow that many of us so strongly associate with Christmas trees.

Many of these ornaments were made for tabletop trees, so they were smaller than those we see today. While I use these on tabletop trees in my own home, these ornaments are now the ones I chose to hang near the top of my trees, as I graduate to larger ones the father down on the tree I'm decorating (more on that in the decorating chapter).

Other early ornaments were paper. Thicker versions were called "Dresden" (hailing originally from that town in Germany, near the Czech Republic) and were typically figures of animals, people, etc. They are often embossed metallic gold and are quite sought after by collectors. Like many desirable ornaments, these are rare because they were often discarded.

Other Dresden ornaments are candy containers that originally held holiday sweets for eager young recipients. These, too, are prized by collectors and can go for hundreds of dollars a piece now.

Other paper ornaments include ones known as "Scraps" and are typically angels and children, and are often glued to a circular spry of spun glass called "Angel Hair." Some are also affixed to wreaths of early lead tinsel and/or wire. There were a few of these in the first box of ornaments I receive from my dad.

Early European (mostly German) scrap ornaments were typically figural ornaments in the shapes of fruit, angels, and Saint Nicholas.

# Before St. Nick Was Jolly

Much has already been written about the evolution of Santa Claus, so I won't attempt to re-tell the story in great detail here. But what I will share is that early versions of the man we've come to know as the brand ambassador for Christmas depict a fellow who was quite serious.

In that first box of ornaments from my dad was one such Santa. When I researched him at the library, I discovered he was known as the "Weihnachtsmann." He wore a long robe and was rather serious, and not at all the ectomorph Santa I'd seen as a child. This early St. Nick was also more serious about the business of naughty versus nice. Weihnachtsmann can be found in all shapes and sizes and is a great addition to any vintage tree.

The ornament I now have used to belong to my German grandmother and was purchased in the 1930s. It still resembles the Weihnachtsmann, "Father Christmas," or "Saint Nicholas" as he's sometimes known. For European immigrants our Santa Claus was still a little foreign for quite some time.

As America began embracing Christmas decorating, it softened and plumped up the German version to become the Santa we know and love. Still it wasn't until the 1940s that Santa emerged on the scene in mercury glass for the tree as we know him today. Even so, European versions stayed true to the Weihnachtsmann image.

Another early German predecessor to Santa Claus was known as the Belsnickle. He, too, is thin, wears a long coat, and is even a bit sinister. As legend had it, he would carry a whip and beat children who were not well behaved. Conversely, he carried sweets and treats that he gave to those children who were good.

Along with German immigrants, the Belsnickle made his way to the US and, thus into Christmas decorations. Most often found in papier-mâché, vintage figures of the Belsnickle were made as ornaments and stand-alone figures—sometimes candy containers. They are often in red robes and carrying small trees. Since they are somewhat rare, originals can also be pricey.

## LIGHT AS A FEATHER

Other early ornaments were much smaller than ones we know today because they were made to adorn the first artificial trees, known as "feather trees," which were literally made of green-dyed goose feathers. They were designed to sit on a tabletop in a parlor—and the ornaments are typical fruits, balls, stars, and other festive shapes.

Larger ornaments from the early twentieth century also still hailed primarily from Europe and are extremely thin and light. They were mouth-blown and hand-painted by artisans who took a great deal of pride in their work. Since they break easily, they are becoming more and more desirable and costly.

## END OF DAY

A slew of serious vintage Christmas collectors are always on the lookout for what are known as "End of Day" ornaments. As the name connotes, they were literally the last pieces artisans would make, and they veered off in a whimsical direction when they did. Using what paints were in front of them, these ornaments are typified by swirled, marbleized detail.

Since End of Day ornaments weren't made for the mass market and often were just made for the workers and their families, they are scarcer than their assembly line cousins. As such, they are pricier too.

"End of day" ornaments

## THE BEAUTY OF AGE

As some ornaments grow older, they lose their paint, and take on an opalescent-luminescent quality. These tend to be some of my favorites. I typically group these ornaments on small, pre-lit white tabletop trees and collectively they take on a pretty magical glow.

I suppose sentimentality places a role in this scenario, as I have no doubt when they were brilliantly colored they were things of wonder for children of all ages. I like the idea that they now have a sublime, wintery second act.

When you think that most of these ornaments are now genuine antiques (over 100 years old), and made of featherweight glass, it's a miracle they are around at all!

## SPUN COTTON, WIRE-WRAPPED, AND ADORNED WITH SCRAPS

Other types of early ornaments include ones made of spun cotton. I have a number of early German spun cotton ornaments in the shape of icicles. They have a sensational, wintery look and by design were sturdy and unbreakable. Other typical spun cotton ornaments include fruits and vegetables and figures such as angels and children. Sometimes they had a printed-paper scrap face.

Speaking of paper scraps, they often adorned more elaborate glass ornaments in the shape of umbrellas, zeppelins, and other fanciful figures. They were typical scraps of paper

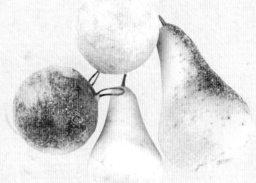

Spun cotton fruit ornaments

with likenesses of angels and cherubs. As a finishing touch, many were wrapped in fine silver wire. These are known as "wire wrapped" ornaments and are prized by collectors.

## PORCELAIN

Some early Japanese ornaments were made of porcelain and were typically bells. They are figural shapes of angels and snowmen and choirboys. Some are in more traditional bell shapes with hand-painted décor. All, however, have one thing in common: They have very sweet rings to them. Still relatively common and inexpensive, I often buy them and tie one to give as a great vintage adornment to the gift, which can also be hung on the recipient's tree.

## HANGERS AND TINSEL

Early hooks for ornaments were not hooks at all . . . but rather pieces of twisted wire. Hooks as we know them today came along much later in the game. Sometimes you'll find vintage ornaments with wire wrapped around the cap, and this is a telltale sign that they are quite old.

Early trees also typically were adorned with icicles and tinsel, which was initially made of silver and then lead, plated with a variety of shiny metals. It's also common to find remnants of it in boxes with old ornaments. Some die-hard collectors still use the old tinsel, but many prefer using its new incarnations that don't contain any trace of lead.

Of course tinsel also came in garland form and the European versions were thinner than the later American counterparts. America manufactured its own tinsel and also twisted colored metal icicles. Both tinsel icicles and metal icicles can be tedious to work with and require a steady hand and patience (a combination that can be challenging to find during the holidays).

## BEADED ORNAMENTS

The Czech people's take on Christmas ornaments came in the form of beaded shapes and designs. Most were in circular shapes with dangling "tails." Others were spider webs (a symbol of good luck) and stars.

Using small to mid-sized mercury glass beads strung on wire, these ornaments are unique and a lovely addition to any vintage tree.

There were a number of these in that first box of ornaments from my dad, so I've been collecting them for a long time. Just as with most ornaments, I'm still finding shapes I never knew existed. Most recently I even found one shaped like a woman's handbag!

## HANDMADE HEIRLOOMS

As tree decorating escalated in popularity in the US, the prices on European glass ornaments made them unavailable to many people. So for households that wanted a tree but couldn't afford ornaments, necessity was the mother of invention.

Early handmade ornaments include paper and cotton batting shapes, including stars, hearts, and other simple, sweet designs. These were often made by the mistress of the house and are now scarce and quite sought after by collectors. The most elaborate example I've seen is a paper ornament adorned with glitter that depicted the gates of Heaven. As you may image, it was pretty heavenly and the price was sky high!

I made this ornament when I was a young boy. I feel the same way today.

Other early handmade decorations included paper chains, most of which didn't survive, and candy, fruit and nuts. Since almost all of these items were perishable, early handmade Christmas is rare and sweet to find.

Handmade ornaments continued in popularity even among households that began to incorporate store-bought ornaments. Often an activity at school or in a family project, handmade ornaments continue to be a holiday staple today.

I made several hundred ornaments when I was a child and we even dedicated one tree to them. Mine were primarily made from kits by a company known as Bucilla and required hand stitching, beading, and embroidery, which my mother taught me.

## BUYING AMERICAN

As I mentioned in the history chapter, as WWII loomed, Americans wanted to buy American, and The Shiny Brite Corporation stepped up to the plate in the Christmas game. Mostly balls, Shiny Brite ornaments where thicker than their European counterparts. They were mass-produced in solid, stripes, and a host of designs, and are often the ones people remember when they think of Christmases past.

My favorite Shiny Brite was also on my German grandmother's tree. It is brilliant purple and says "Silent Night" in white painted lettering along with images of the wise men following the Star of Bethlehem. This ornament is by no means rare, and should only cost $1 to $3 at a flea market, but to me it holds great emotional value.

After WWII broke out, America needed to use many of the resources that were being put into Christmas ornaments for the war effort. So the metal caps and silvering inside the ornaments that gave them their hallmark sheen quickly disappeared.

Un-silvered ornaments with paper caps were the result. In some cases ornaments were un-silvered and included a small piece of tinsel to add sheen, and in others they have a crude cutoff in the glass with a simple piece of wire inserted.

For me, these ornaments always take a place of honor on my trees. They are tangible reminders of how the war touched all aspects of life and how everyone came together for the common good. I'm not alone in my love of WWII American ornaments, and many of my fellow patriotic collectors have many of these in their collections.

## FANTASTIC PLASTIC

As plastics were developed to aid the war effort, they also emerged as materials for Christmas ornaments. Often found in red, white, and blue, the first plastic ornaments were typically in the shapes of stars, angels, and bells, with other figures coming in later years to include choirboys, snowmen, and

# "Every Time a Bell Rings, An Angel Gets His Wings"

When little Zuzu utters that now famous line from the end of my favorite holiday film *It's a Wonderful Life*, there's a little silver bell ringing on the Bailey's Christmas tree. That little bell and so many others like it were made of aluminum and often painted gold, red, and green. Typically Japanese, these bells were popular because they had a great look to them and a great sound. I always have a number of them on my tree, and try to put them near the tips of lower branches, so they may let out a ring or two as people pass by. I also enjoy tying them with ribbon and adding them to holiday packages.

St. Nick. I love many of plastic ornaments because they come to life in a big way when exposed to the lights on the tree.

Of course the biggest selling point of plastic ornaments was their durability. Advertised as "unbreakable," plastic ornaments were safer for families with small children and pets and didn't create messes to clean up. Completely aligned with dawn of the Atomic Age, many shapes went from traditional to exaggerated. America was ready for something new, and plastic ornaments answered the call. Some of my favorites include sputniks, chandeliers, and tops.

One of the leaders in the world of plastic ornaments was the Bradford Novelty Company of Boston, Massachusetts. Chances are if you find a shiny vintage plastic ornament that resembles silvered glass, then you have found a Bradford ornament.

Another pioneer in post-war plastics was the Tinkle Toy Company (a division of Plakie Toys) of Youngstown, Ohio. In 1950 they came up with one of the most iconic plastic ornaments ever made: The Christmas Tree Twinkler. Shaped like a carousel (although some say a bird cage), each had a little propeller inside that spun when it was exposed to the heat of Christmas tree lights. Also called "spinners" by many who remember them, these came in very 1950s colors like watermelon, turquoise, and

chartreuse. The part with the colored plastic also had glitter mixed in the plastic. The propellers were contained inside a clear center portion to offer optimal viewing of the spinning action. Their marketing materials promised "whirling, twirling perpetual action." What kid wouldn't want to see that on his or her tree?

Spinners really spun best when the were hung directly above a vintage light. Of course some got too close to the light bulb, so often you find warped or somewhat melted spinners on the vintage market today.

At our family business we had spinners on the tree in the front window. They seemed to perfectly color coordinate with the neon sign bearing our name. My guess is that when my grandparents bought them to put in the window, they were all the rage.

I remember always being a little perplexed by them as a kid because they looked like they should move, but they didn't. Now I realize it's because at some point we switched over to small, clear modern lights, which never gave off enough heat to get the spinners going. It wasn't until I began collecting that I understood the scenario.

Today plastic spinners are the most highly collected and pricey of the plastic ornaments on the market. My guess is because so many people have fun childhood memories attached to them . . . and because many that warped or melted were discarded.

As popular as plastic ornaments became (and still are today), they never replaced traditional glass ornaments. Many who are vintage and antique Christmas purists don't include any plastic ornaments on their trees and even cap off their collection at the early 1940s. As for me, I think they add something of value historically and I like the way the look mixed with their older glass comrades.

## EPHEMERAL ORNAMENTS

As I mentioned, some of the first European ornaments were made with embossed paper scraps. These were typically angels and were wildly popular in the Victorian era.

During WWII, America also made paper ornaments for the same rationale as mentioned above. All the most valuable resources were being put to use, so paper ornaments emerged in a variety of shapes and sizes. My favorite wartime paper ornaments in my collection are by Merri-Lei and still have their original box (an incredible find!) and are in the figures of an army and a navy officer, a battleship, and other military figures as well as figures depicting what they were fighting for back on the home front—a baby carriage, a rocking horse, etc.

Other favorite paper ornaments I've got in my collection were giveaways from companies or cutouts from magazines. I particularly like an embossed paper set that came inside a bag of flower. To add to the vintage appeal, I even have the original sleeve they came in when they were tucked in the bag. We vintage Christmas nerds love stuff like that.

## POST-WAR OPTIMISM

After WWII, the economy improved and just about every house that celebrated Christmas had a tree. All those trees required a great deal of ornaments. So more and more companies began to emerge, but Shiny Brite continued to reign supreme for a good, long time.

New shapes and colors began to emerge including Sputniks as outlined in the plastics section earlier, and other signs of the Atomic Age. More and more plastics and other materials that were developed for the war effort also emerged in ornaments. Christmas had become big business.

## LET IT GLOW

In yet another technological advancement twist glow-in-the-dark ornaments also emerged on the scene. Both paper and plastic, I've seen everything from icicles to snowmen. When used together in a large number, they still create quite a cool impact.

Everything from disco balls to gingham sachets adorned trees. Some took on themes or color schemes that reflected changing tastes.

## ENTER THE "KEEPSAKE"

Companies like Hallmark branded ornaments "Keepsake" and others liberally used words like "Heirloom." As such, there is a dizzying array of vintage Christmas out there for the picking.

Keep in mind that "vintage" literally means twenty years or older, so if you're now an adult, chances are décor you recall from your childhood is now vintage. How scary is that?

While the proliferation of types of ornaments created lots of different trees, the ones I always like best are the ones with ornaments that look as if they were collected over time. My trees are very much like this. Some of my ornaments are as early as the late 1800s and others are only a few decades old, but somehow it works.

My taste is decidedly maximal and nostalgic. Thank goodness for me and for all of you out there who want to start collecting, there is no shortage of wonderful vintage ornaments. So dive in and enjoy!

## STANDS

Since the days of the very first Christmas trees, there was a need for stands to hold them in place and provide a reservoir for water to keep them alive. The earliest German stands were made of cast iron to provide substantial weight to help the tree not to tip over. Later materials included aluminum and plastic.

Hallmark began making its mark on the ornament market in the 1970s. This Tiny Tim rag doll could be a package decoration or an ornament. It retains its original card with Tim's famous line from *A Christmas Carol*: "God Bless Us Every One."

Tree stands have earned their rightful place in the antique and vintage Christmas collecting arena. One of my favorites includes an early electrified stand with light bulbs and outlets to plug in the tree lights. It is painted green and gold and because it has lights of its own, it is, by design, part of the overall décor. Another favorite is a 1950s aluminum stand with jolly snowmen painted on it. It, too, was meant to be seen as part of the décor.

Made by the Coloramic Company, this cheerful 1950s Christmas tree stand is a great example of how American companies began to envision every aspect of the tree as decorative.

A cast iron German Christmas tree stand made for a tabletop feather tree. Since it was at eye-level, it was decorative as well. I purchased this one at an antiques shop in Frankfurt.

For a while I even had a stand that revolved and played Christmas music, but became a bit more like a carnival attraction and less like a Christmas tree, so I eighty-sixed it. That said, the one thing it did well was showcase my collection from every angle!

As stands became less decorative and more utilitarian, tree skirts entered the scene. Because of the size and weight of my largest tree, I use a new, heavy-duty stand but I put vintage fabric around it. Some also choose to put a blanket of cotton batting under the tree to resemble snow.

## UNDER THE TREE

Growing up in a German family, I had what's known as a "putz" or piece of wood that went under the tree and tree stand where I'd have my train set, houses, and a whole wonderland village. While its roots may have been in Germany, America ran with the electric train and all of its trimmings for a world of wonder that began happening under the Christmas tree. Track, locomotives, cars of every shape and color, tunnels, houses, trees, people, animals, and more were manufactured and became big business. This is now an entire subset of Christmas collecting and is sure to bring out the kid in everyone.

Also commonly found under the tree were lead figures of ice skaters and skiers. I grew up with ice skaters on round and oval mirrors that resembled frozen ponds. Needless to say a world of imagination took place under the tree, and for vintage enthusiasts like me, it still does!

As a collector of antiques and vintage items, I often place things like dollhouses, windup cars, and other things that may once have been under a tree long ago, under mine.

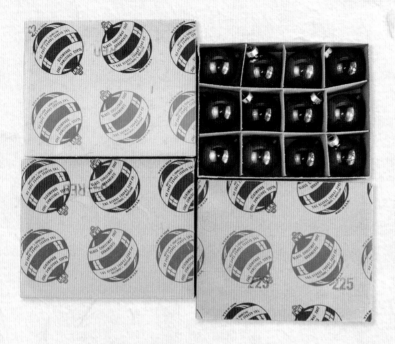

These American-made ornaments were likely 5 and 10 Cent store purchases. The George Franke Sons Company was out of Baltimore, Maryland, and aimed to give Shiny Brite some healthy competition. Made in the early 1950s, these may have been the only color ornament on the tree. At the time it became popular to have a monochromatic look.

Depending on how much I've got going on under the tree any given year, I also place my crèche or nativity scene there. It can take on a beautiful glow with all of the lights and other décor.

## REPRODUCTION ALERT!

Many European glass molds for figural ornaments are being used to create new versions of old ornaments. I don't believe the intention of these ornaments is to fool people, but that can be the result. I have no qualms with new ornaments made in the old style. In fact I often like these ornaments very much and own several myself. They are sold in fine stores and still made in the same manner as they were 100 years ago.

The only problem with these new "Heirloom" or "Old World" ornaments is one of mistaken identity. The surest way to know if an ornament is old is to look at the cap on top. If it shows age, the ornament is likely old. If it is bright and shiny, it is likely new. Also, many of the reproductions have the wire hanger part in a star shape, while old ornaments just have a loop of wire.

Other obvious ways to spot a reproduction is to look at the overall brightness and luster of the paint. If it looks too perfect and brilliant, it is likely new. Know what you're buying and buy what you like!

## BUYER BEWARE

It just goes to stand that the more valuable an antique or vintage ornament is, the more likely it is to be reproduced. As I mentioned at the beginning of the chapter, German and French kugels have become quite expensive, so a whole crop of new kugels have been produced in India, and caps are chemically "aged" to fool the eye. In addition to being faux aged on the cap, these new kugels also seem to have an intentional crackling on the surface as well. A great way to not get fooled is to look them up online and train your eye to be on alert for fakes.

Like the previous chapter, my aim here is to educate and empower collectors to know what to look for out there and train their eyes to zoom in on items they like when scanning stalls of flea markets and other venues.

Vintage ornaments are found in every imaginable material and color. This pipe cleaner snowflake and cotton batting Santa are a couple examples.

The Holy Family comes in many shapes and sizes and is made of every imaginable material. This simple chalkware set is from the 1950s and is on my coffee table every year.

A porcelain baby Jesus made in Japan. Like most all of my pieces, he's a flea market find. Each year he spends Christmas on my dining room table.

These small glittered Japanese cardboard ornaments were usually in the forms of houses or stables like the one shown here. They could either stand freely in a display or hang on the tree. I do both things with them.

The vibrant colors of these 1920s glittered cardboard ornaments make them both rare and appealing. It looks as if they were never used. The doll carriage, rocking horse, wagon, and drum perfectly resemble gifts that may be under the tree. I always thought these would be great on a tree in a child's room.

This box is shown as it was presented to me by my friend Armand. He scours estate sales that I can't always attend and finds wonderful things for me. Most of these are over 100 years old, so they officially cross the line from vintage to antique. I treasure them and usually pack them away at the end of the year in the same box he gave me.

This box of German tinsel and mercury glass ornaments is telling me everything I needed to know to date it. One of the ornaments has the date on it of 1918. It's possible this date was pulled from a calendar and added to the tinsel, or was there originally. At the time, many ornaments were wrapped in wire and/or tinsel and had paper, silk, and other materials attached to them.

When WWII came along, precious resources were rationed. As a result many American Christmas ornaments from this time ceased adding silvering to the inside of balls, and used paper hangers and caps instead of their usual metal ones.

These colorful 1970s teardrop ornaments were distributed by the Liberty Bell company, which ironically enough had them manufactured in Columbia.

These wonderful mercury glass ornaments are in their original store boxes. I love the way they look here almost as much as I love the way they look on the tree. I was told by the vendor that these were "new old stock," meaning they were taken from an old store's stockroom, and likely never used.

Tinsel garlands are wrapped around trees for an extra layer of sparkle. Early German versions are made of lead alloy, but later American incarnations are made of cellophane and other non-toxic materials.

This small box of ornaments was the perfect size for a feather or tabletop tree. Today I use small ornaments like this to fill in little holes or near the top of my large tree.

This small bottlebrush wreath was likely sold at Woolworths or another Five and Dime. Like many pieces of holiday merchandise sold at such stores, it had multiple uses. Often pieces adorned packages, and then the recipient began using them as tree ornaments.

—◦◦————————————————◦◦—

There are vintage Christmas ornaments for every imaginable taste and vision. These 1960s examples could come together to create a tree that would be very much in the pink. The frosted balls look like sugared candy and the angel hair could be either used on or under the tree.

This multicolored bottlebrush star features a foil rosette with small mercury glass balls and American Flags. I love vintage patriotic decorations like this.

Here are Victorian ornaments that have lost much of their original color. I think this gives them a different kind of beauty that really comes to life on a tree. Since much of their external color is lost, more of their internal shine comes through.

These 1950s star ornaments remind me of women's jewelry that was popular in that era. They may have once adorned a tree in a department store. Now I hang them on a mirror in my hallway.

As long as I've been collecting, I still find things I've never seen before. This is because there were countless ornaments made. It's always a treat when I make a new discovery, like these early German starburst ornaments I found. The colors and detail are pretty sensational.

The Victorians loved floral forms and ornaments. This selection is a typical array from the early 1900s.

Wintery white ornaments are some of my very favorites. The owl's white upper body adds a magical touch to one of my favorite forms. The clip on tree looks like a snow-covered evergreen.

This Czech mercury glass locomotive set inside a thin red glass circle is both sweet and uncommon.

Strings of mercury glass beads were a popular touch for trees for many years. This small string of red and silver beads is from the early 1900s.

Vintage ornaments come in every size, shape and color. This grouping of 1940s American ornaments is in fun, punchy colors, and when placed on the tree, have a candy-like look to them.

This ornament appealed to me on many levels. I love pink decorations; I always look for WWII unsilvered examples, and I love that someone used a string to hang it on the tree. Ornaments are really a snapshot of history—if you look closely. This one reminds me that people made do with what they had and even in lean times, celebrated Christmas.

Another ornament in the original box from my dad, this Victorian ice cream cone is an example of an ornament that was often the favorite of little ones.

Musical instruments were popular forms in the early 1900s. While horns are the most common, I've amassed a nice collection of string instruments, like this long white cello.

Clip-on birds with spun glass tails are favorites for many collectors. Some decorate trees with only bird ornaments. I try to evenly disperse mine throughout my trees. I find adding these last is the way to go, since they can often be placed where hanging ornaments don't fit as easily.

Mercury glass candy canes are typically in red and green, so this pink one is a special find. It's made extra special by the addition of a little spun cotton mushroom and a bow. Like many ornaments, this may have originally adorned a gift. These candy canes can be hung on the tree like real candy canes. Since this one is pretty unique, I often display it on a side table in one of my vignettes.

Tinsel and spun glass were common materials to showcase Victorian paper scraps. Like mercury glass, they both reflect the light on a tree beautifully. At the time these were made, that light was from candles.

For some reason, the Japanese ornaments in my collection tend to be primarily pink or green, or a combination of the two. I think I am really drawn to their particular take on these colors. These two sizable 1930s pinecones were finds on a recent trip to Seattle.

Foil ornaments like these became popular in the 1950s and 1960s because they were as reflective as glass, but didn't break.

Midcentury plastic spinner ornaments like this one were heat-activated, so when placed near a light bulb, the pinwheel in the middle would actually spin. Many got too close to hot lights, however, so you often find them partially melted. These are prized by collectors and often on the pricier side of vintage ornaments out there.

I bought this vintage Italian tomato when it was new in the 1980s. Back then when I began collecting I bought more new ornaments and this one has been a favorite for about thirty Christmases now.

Foil ice cream cones like these are common flea market finds. I think they look best when they are displayed in larger collections.

The fun, punchy colors of these 1940s ornaments are reminiscent of candy. While not the quintessential "Christmas colors," these are favorites of mine because they are so joyful.

This sweet 1960s skater felt ornament has a lot of charm. It's another example of a vintage kid-friendly ornament.

I found these fun 1950s Styrofoam ornaments in Santa Fe. Since they are not fragile, they were easy vintage souvenirs to bring home from my trip.

This twisted snow-capped icicle is large and lovely. On the tree it has great presence, and the shape really stands out in the crowd.

Ornaments from certain time periods reflect the tastes and styles of the era. In Victorian times, ladies often carried parasols, so there were lots of parasol ornaments made. This large example looks great near other ornaments made at the same time, like this small, but elaborate bowl of fruit and this wire-wrapped ball.

Hearts are another popular form for vintage tree ornaments. This pink "quilted" German one is a favorite of mine.

Mercury glass ornaments are silvered inside and painted on the outside, so they really dance in the light of a Christmas tree. They really come to life when assembled in groups. The more the merrier!

Patriotic ornaments are very popular with collectors. This red, white, and blue ball is a classic example.

Mercury glass candy canes were made in the likeness of their real-life confectionary counterparts. They could be hung on the tree just like real candy canes. I also think they look great displayed in bowls or on trays.

---

Wire-wrapped ornaments were popular on early Christmas trees. The tinsel added to the overall shine. This example is especially nice because the ornament has such a fun hand-painted pattern.

---

The oldest bells in the late 1800s and early 1900s generally had a wire with a small bead that was a clapper, which made the bell gently ring. These three early German bells are favorites of mine. The ones on either end are from the original box given to me by my dad.

This early German moth ornament has spun glass wings. When originally made, it likely had a metal clip for affixing it to the tree (similar to the ones on bird ornaments). It was lost over the years, so someone tied a string around it to hang. This actually makes me love this ornament even more . . . because someone appreciated it enough to find a new way to display it.

The Irwin Company manufactured many celluloid versions of Santa. My favorite is this unusual egg-shaped ornament.

The satin-like off-white sheen of this ornament gives it a special glow when it's on the tree and the shooting star motif is a favorite of mine.

Nature was frequently represented in Christmas ornament form. This fancy silver leaf with golden acorns is from West Germany.

* * *

The fun mod lines of this tree-shaped ornament reflect how tastes were changing in mid-twentieth-century America. Made with classic materials, it offered up a new take on an old form.

* * *

This sweet unsilvered ball is hand painted and a piece of tinsel inside gives it a bit of shimmer.

* * *

Fancy, detailed blown glass ornaments with arms like this one are true works of art. Because of this (and because they are so easily breakable), they are prized by collectors.

In the 1980s, *The Snowman* became a popular animated special on PBS. Adapted from the book by Raymond Briggs, it tells the story of a young boy and his snowman who comes to life. All done with music in lieu of words, it is a joy to watch and I highly recommend it. After it became a bit of a sensation, Royal Doulton created porcelain items with images from the special. These four were given to me by my sister when I was quite young. Every year they take a place of honor among my Christmas décor, and every year I still watch *The Snowman*.

The Barclay company was a leader in manufacturing lead figural toys in the 1920s through the 1950s. Some of their most popular figures were these ice skaters, which were often displayed in large winter scenes on mirrored ponds. Skiers were also very popular, often displayed on cotton bating "snow."

In Germany, the "putz" was often as important as the tree. An entire world of people and buidings, it typically included a train set as well. I grew up with a putz in my home as a child and I could get lost for hours in the little world I created in it. These wooden figures were handmade in Germany in the early 1900s.

# CHAPTER 4

# Lights

As soon as Christmas trees came on the scene, people wanted to light them. As I mentioned in the history chapter, the earliest way Christmas trees were lit were with actual candles. Since this was both potentially hazardous and costly, trees were often light on Christmas Eve and/or Christmas day for short periods.

Early candles were held in place with metal clips and holders, which are still widely collected. Sometimes the clips were weighted with clay or metal balls or even with a glass ornament to mitigate the risk of the candle tipping over.

Many collectors who still use candles do so on small tabletop feather trees or artificial trees. The result can be quite beautiful but still hazardous and a lot of work!

Even though the advent of electricity changed tree lighting forever, the crossover was gradual, since many households didn't even have electricity until the 1940s. Once people made the switch, however, for the majority there was no turning back.

## CHRISTMAS ELECTRIFIED

In the early days of electric Christmas lights, the wiring was the stuff of many holiday headaches. Wires often became tangled and would take a long time to get out of knots. In addition, early strings took more energy so circuits often blew. To add insult to injury, if one bulb in any given string went out, so did the rest of them. Once a tree was decorated, this became even more challenging!

All these barriers aside, once the soft glow of electric bulbs began illuminating trees, all bets were off. Everyone wanted them. The primary colors took on an almost neon sign glow and intensified the luminesce of the silvered glass ornaments. Unlike candles, electric lights would be left on for long periods of time so the soft glow of Christmas was here to stay.

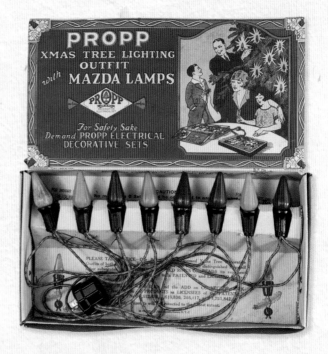

These colored lights were initially a cone shape, which was later replaced by a larger, rounded bulb that most people remember from their grandparent's trees. My grandmother had such bulbs and I remember how the glow her tree gave off was pretty mesmerizing for me.

## REFLECTORS

To intensify the glow, tin and aluminum reflectors in starburst shapes were created. They could be put between the bulb and the socket and resembled a sort of outer space flower. Reflectors came in boxes sold separately from the lights and were silver as well as varying shades of metallic colors.

Many collectors use vintage multicolored lights (and reflectors) to achieve an authentic vintage look. Some years I've decorated my own trees with vintage lights and reflectors and the look is warm, nostalgic, and joyful.

## AND...THEY'RE BLINKING!

As technology advanced, so did lighting. Lights were now made that could blink—and adapters were also sold to turn your already existing lights into "blinkers." I flirted with blinking lights for a brief time in my early days of tree decorating . . . but I felt like they were one toe over the line for me. As much as I'm a maximalist with décor, I enjoy looking at it all in a way that feels Zen to me . . . and blinking lights just didn't fit in that scenario!

## FIGURAL LIGHTS

Milk glass figural lights were sort of a combination ornament and light. Made in many, many shapes and hand-painted, these lights are still prized by collectors. Santas, angels, birds, starbursts, and bells—the list goes on and on—these bulbs were initially made in Germany using actual ornament molds. As they increased in popularity, Japan began producing them as well. Now when collectors find them, many have lost a bit of paint, but are still desirable. Even the ones that no longer work are collected. Because they are so charming, people often tie bows to or wrap wire around the screw part and use them as ornaments.

## BUBBLE LIGHTS

Perhaps one of the most nostalgic vintage Christmas lights of all is the bubble light. Introduced in 1946 by NOMA, bubble lights were the perfect addition to the post-war American tree. Each bulb contained a tube of colored liquid that began to bubble when the plastic saucer shape beneath it (which contained a light bulb) began to warm.

Similar in shape to a candle and candleholder from the earliest trees, bubble lights were ultra-modern and ultra-fun. In addition to illuminating, they also add movement and another dimension to tree decorating. In order to keep the bubble light upright, wooden beads were pulled through the wire to create a snug fit on a tree's branches. Metal clips were also used to keep them upright, which was key because a bubble light off to its side not only looks out of place—it won't bubble.

I began collecting bubble lights early on and have amassed a nice assortment of them now. I don't always use them on my trees, but I do have several lit in special candoliers that were made to hold them. To me, nothing says vintage Christmas like bubble lights in action!

Bubble lights as found at a flea market.

## COLOR WHEEL

As aluminum trees became popular in the late 1950s and 1960s, a new idea in tree lighting emerged: the color wheel. Literally a rotating wheel with Mylar inserts in primary colors, it would sit beneath the tree and illuminate it. As the wheel would turn, the tree would transform into each color. Color wheels and the aluminum trees they illuminated were considered ultra-modern at the time and came in and out of popularity in a relatively short period of time.

It's interesting to note that aluminum trees were first designed as store displays and then were produced for consumers. While they were most commonly made in silver, they were also produced in colors including pink, teal, gold, red, and baby blue.

When I began collecting vintage Christmas I had little interest in an aluminum tree, but in recent years I've come to appreciate the place it holds in history. Perhaps I had been turned against them by *A Charlie Brown Christmas*, which suggested they were cold and too commercial. Charlie Brown's humble evergreen just needed a little love and it was the embodiment of The Christmas Spirit. That said, for interiors with Midcentury Modern furniture, these trees and their mod color wheels are ideal. I had one in my office and it was frequent topic of conversation and amusement.

## LIGHTED ICE, SNOWBALLS, AND MORE

Just as ornaments took on so many shapes, sizes, and designs, so did lights. Other favorites of mine are the "snowball" and "lighted ice" bulbs made by GE. In white and a variety of colors, these bulbs are flocked with "snow" and take on a look that feels both whimsical and nostalgic. Other shapes include Chinese lanterns, icicles, and yes, even chili peppers!

## CLEAR LIGHTS

The small white lights that are common today didn't really emerge on the scene until the 1970s. Now rather ubiquitous, I actually use these lights on the largest of my trees. I find that since I use so many ornaments, they don't fight for the limelight, but rather create a serene backdrop. I also like these lights because they are cool to the touch and I feel confident using literally thousands of them on my trees without worrying about overloading circuits.

Some of my tabletop trees are also pre-lit, which saves time and allows me to focus more on the part I enjoy: decorating!

## LIGHTED FIGURES AND CANDOLIERS

As Christmas decorating electrified, not only the tree was illuminated. Mantles, windowsills, side tables—you name it, were all now areas to be adorned. Oh and don't forget on top of the television! Lighted figures included Santas and snowmen, angels and wreaths. I had a large plastic Santa in my bedroom as a child (my brother put it there when he surprised me with that decorated tree). It doubled as a night-lite and gave a warm, seasonal glow to my room.

Another favorite indoor figure of mine was made in the early 1930s by Cheer-o-Lite, and is a decidedly Art Deco frosted metal cone with glitter on its surface. It has cut-out geometric shapes filled with colored Mylar. A light bulb inside brings it all to life.

I've also got a Cheer-o-Lite wreath made in the same fashion. It was a find my friend Armand put aside for me. He found it in an old estate in New York and it retains its original box with a 1934 date on it. On the box, the former owner wrote, "For the dining room." So naturally I put it in my dining room each year.

Other indoor lighting included electrified candoliers, which were placed in the windows and on the mantles. Some even included plastic "halos" to add to the thrill of electric candelabrum.

## SAFETY FIRST

A word of caution about vintage lighting . . . because they are older electrical items, they can potentially be a fire hazard. Never leave a tree lit when you are not home and if wiring on old lights seems questionable, it's best to pass them by. The truth is, while I love vintage lighting, on most of my own trees I use new lights for safety reasons and because, given the scale of my largest trees, new lights are easier to work with.

## REPRODUCTION ALERT!

Just as with vintage ornaments, some vintage lights have been reproduced. There's nothing wrong with purchasing them for a vintage look, but know what you are buying. Figural milk glass lights were reproduced as well as bubble lights. As with ornaments, it's best to let your eye be your guide. If the paint is brilliant and the screws show no wear, then they are likely new.

"Christmas is doing
A LITTLE SOMETHING
EXTRA for someone."
—CHARLES M. SCHULZ

Christmas lights came in many shapes and sizes. I found these early cone-shaped, mulitcolored light bulbs in this brick lithograph box at the flea market. I always keep a box of them around at the holidays, since when it comes to early electric lighting . . . if one bulb goes out, the whole string goes out.

Christmas lighting continued to be reinvented over the years, with different colors and shapes routinely introduced. These boxes of lights from "Glo-Ray" offered larger, round multicolored bulbs, which mirrored the look and feel of ornaments.

Since Christmas lights often burned out—and when one went out, the entire set went out—it was key to have a box of extras on hand like this box of bulbs from Westinghouse.

The leaping reindeer and stylized trees adorning this box of Reliance Christmas tree lights are decidedly Art Deco. I like the box even more than the lights themselves.

Two boxes of early electric Christmas tree lights from Reliance and Propp. The graphics on each make them highly collectible and attractive to display.

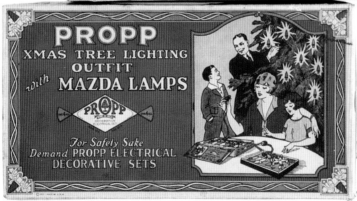

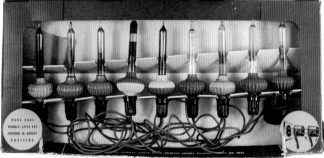

For many, the mesmerizing incandescent glow of bubble lights epitomize vintage Christmas. This iconic box from NOMA is probably the most recognized set. Bubble lights came on the scene in 1946 and their joyful presence was the perfect thing for post-war American homes. While the first out of the gate with these, NOMA didn't keep the patent, so other companies followed with their own versions of bubbling lights in subsequent years.

Another variation on the NOMA box, the multicolored plastic bases and oil create a look that's both joyful and nostalgic.

Another company to manufacture bubble lights, Yule-Glo depicted Santa and his sleigh orbiting their product.

As tree lighting technology advanced, companies created devices like this "Flasher" which caused them to blink when plugged into a standard light set. This one retains its original packing card, which lets consumers know they can disregard the smoke that may appear as a result after the first use!

Inside the pages of the Maspback Incorporated 1949 Toy Catalog I found this "Royalite 9 Lite Bubbling Candelite," which I own and happily display in my living room. It's fun to see pieces in my collection as they were originally sold.

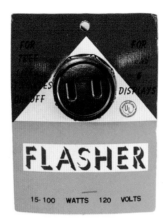

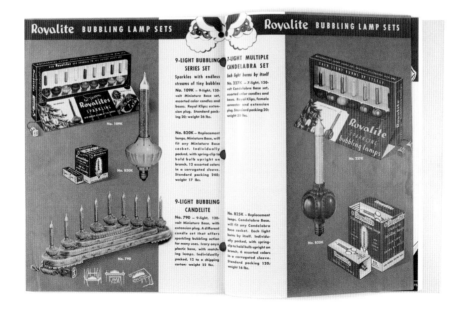

Probably the most recognized light bulb shape, this red light set gives off a pretty magical glow. It also emanates a lot more heat than today's light sets.

Some fancier Christmas tree candleholders have figural ornaments attached to them. The benefit was two-fold: The ornaments were decorative and they provided a bit of weight and balance so the candle wouldn't tip over. This one from the early 1900s has lost much of its color but is still quite lovely when displayed on the tree.

These Paramount Star Light Lights were popular mid-century alternatives to the standard bulbs. This assortment shows their various shapes, sizes, and colors.

Many early Christmas lights were what are referred to as "figural," which means they are in the shapes of Santas, birds, stars, and a million other things. They were made of milk glass and were really like glowing ornaments. This set is in its original box.

These early figural milk glass light bulbs from the 1920s and 1930s hail from Germany and Japan. They were sold individually and as sets. Even when these no longer work, I enjoy displaying them in bowls or tying a ribbon around the base and using them as ornaments on the tree.

To add pizazz to Christmas lights, these plastic stars were manufactured. The light bulb would screw into the base as usual, but these were sandwiched in between. The result was a wonderful glow—and in the case of these, a very patriotic one.

This early electric tree topper had the same cone-shaped bulbs many people had on their tree. To switch things up, lights could be varied in color, or people could choose a monochromatic look like the one here in blue.

This old German lantern once held a candle that made the thin translucent panels glow. It was a fancy alternative to a simple clip-on candleholder. Often hung in groups, dispersed throughout a tree, these are quite magical. It's rare to find them without damage, so I was delighted when my friend Armand presented me with this one.

This colorful slide shows an idyllic wintery scene. Made for Victorian parlor versions of View Masters, these slides provided entertainment before TV. Today they are very collectible.

CHAPTER

# 5

# Outdoor Décor

## IT STARTS AT THE FRONT DOOR

The traditional Christmas wreath was the first piece of holiday décor to make it outdoors. A front door staple, the wreath took on many incarnations over the years, and was often embellished with lights and other decorations.

Still the most popular piece of outdoor décor—and easiest to pull off, wreaths pre-date Christmas and have Pagan roots. A universal sign of welcome, wreaths can run the gamut from humble to extravagant. I usually buy my wreaths first from a florist or tree farms. The evergreen variety last for a long time outside and other versions fabricated from manmade and natural materials are everlasting and a holiday staple.

One of my favorite wreaths is made from artichoke leaves that were glued to a Styrofoam mold. The entire thing was spray-painted gold. I hang it with a black ribbon on a black door and the look is quite striking and elegant.

That said, I also always have a number of evergreen wreaths because they are truly timeless. I often adorn mine with oranges and dried pomegranates and wrap them with ribbon. I say show your individuality and be creative with your wreaths. From fruits and greens to illuminated versions with neon and flashing lights . . . the wreath is here to stay.

Americans, however, didn't stop at the front door. As technology advanced in the mid-twentieth century, outdoor lights became commonplace and a truly American take on decorating. What started with stores and other businesses eventually crossed over to residential communities.

## MORE IS MORE

Rooftops, trees, mailboxes, and walkways became illuminated and entire neighborhoods joined in on the fun. Some even engaged in a bit of healthy competition with their neighbors as they tried to outdo each other. This still goes on today and there are some neighborhoods that look more like Las Vegas than Anytown, USA.

As I grew older and expanded my interest in vintage Christmas beyond the tree, outside was a whole new frontier. I began going to auctions and yard sales and finding wonderful outdoor lights for pennies on the dollar. In those early years I experimented with many combinations (multicolored, all white, gold, etc.). My favorite combination became blue and green. There was something about that cool glow that really did it for me.

Much larger than indoor bulbs, I found outdoor bulbs naturally gave off twice the amount of radiance. I alternated blue and green bulbs and strung them along the perimeters of the roof, the door, and the windows. I also managed to wrangle a few industrial extension cords and adorned two evergreen trees in the front yard.

All of these lights eventually went into one source—the light on the ceiling of the front porch. With one flick of the light switch in the front hall, the front of our house was a glowing masterpiece (well at least I thought so!).

As you may gather from reading the above, outdoor lighting can be a lot of work and serious decorators start as early as Halloween.

## A CANDLE IN EVERY WINDOW

Another look that very much appeals to me, and is much easier to pull off than the above scenario, is a simple candle in every window. In the early days of decorating this way, a plastic candle with a bulb was literally placed in every window . . . and had to be plugged and unplugged every evening to a nearby power outlet. I know this because as I kid I tried it. As a result, there were many evenings that the candles never did make it on!

Luminaries in Santa Fe, New Mexico.

I've since discovered that there were some early battery-operated models that would have made this look easier to pull off. Thanks to advances in technology, new battery-operated light candles that flicker are now on the market. As much as I love all things vintage, if a vintage look with a bit of a twist is available, I'm all in!

## LUMINARIES

Another really sublime outdoor lighting solution are simple brown bags filled with sand and tea lights. They often line the walk of a home and create a serene, inviting look. It has a decidedly Southwest look and some of my most beautiful memories of seeing them were on a trip to Santa Fe, New Mexico. Again, technology has advanced such that battery-operated tea lights can be used in lieu of traditional ones.

## BLOW MOLD FIGURES

The large plastic electrified figures often seen on front lawns across America are known largely as "blow mold" figures. Santa and his reindeer, the Holy Family, carolers, etc. all became popular outdoor lighting accessories. Most of them were on the lawn, but often Santa and his team made their way to the roof as well.

One of the most popular and ubiquitous examples of blow mold decorations are large red candles with yellow flames. We had them on my front porch when I was growing up and I know lots of others who did as well.

Blow mold figures certainly evoke a million memories for so many people and are a great addition to your outdoor vintage vignette. Due to their large size but light weight, sometimes a figure would blow away if not properly weighted and many have memories of the baby Jesus or Santa winding up in

the street or the neighbor's yard. Given this, I always recommend weighting them with sand (that's what we did with our blow mold candles many moons ago).

## WOODEN FIGURES

My favorite piece of outdoor décor, I found at a flea market. It is a hand-painted life-size wooden figure of Santa Claus. I imagine someone made it back in the days when most American homes had workshops in the basement. I know mine did!

Probably made in the late 1940s, my Santa comes to life when one spotlight is shined on him. Made of simple plywood, he's still quite merry and colorful and his hand is lifted in a waving position to greet passersby. Handmade lawn pieces like this are sometimes best found at estate and tag sales. They are very vintage and very sweet.

The house across the street from us when I was growing up always had a piece of plywood with the Three Wiseman following the star painted on it in a mural fashion. They, too, had one simple spotlight shining on it, and the look was simple but profound.

## SANTA'S RIDE

I've seen just about everything adoring people's lawns but one of the most memorable was an actual sleigh from the early nineteenth century. Filled with boxes wrapped with Mylar paper and adorned with bows . . . and illuminated with a spotlight, the sleigh really looks like Santa dropped by and came inside to leave presents and have a few cookies.

## FOR THE BIRDS

One of the sweetest ways to decorate outdoors also treats our fine-feathered friends to some sustenance. An ideal craft project for the younger members of the family, the materials are simple: pinecones, string, peanut butter, and birdseed. First tie string to the tops of the pinecones. Then roll the cones in peanut butter (or ice them with a rubber spatula), and roll them in birdseed. As a child I created these and enjoyed decorating a tree in the backyard with them.

Every morning and afternoon I'd watch as the birds came to feed. It's a project that requires minimal time and effort and offers a feel-good result. While often reserved for children, I did this as an adult at my country home and found it deeply enjoyable. There were a steady succession of birds and it felt like I was providing a valuable offering for them.

## ANYTHING GOES

Nowadays there are a host of outdoor lights and lighted figures that require minimal effort—like inflatable lit figures of Winnie the Pooh and Santa and icicle lights. To each his own, but for me these are too newfangled. I prefer the vintage vibes I mentioned above. That said, in a few years these things will be vintage too . . . so it's all relative!

# CHAPTER 6

# Putting It All Together

## DECORATING *WITH* VINTAGE CHRISTMAS

or many, the holiday season officially begins when the tree is decorated. What's a joy for some is a drudgery for others, Clearly I fall in the joy camp and chances are if you're reading this, you do too. In this chapter I'll offer some thoughts, advice, anecdotes, and inspiration on all things related to trimming the tree.

## PLANNING

Just as you do when a guest comes to your home, it's important to clean and clear the space (or spaces) where your tree (or trees) will go. For apartment dwellers, this can be a challenging time that often calls for creativity and compromise. For example, in my New York City apartment, I routinely move a large chair from my living room into my bedroom, which results in me not being able to access my closet easily. This kind of compromise is a no-brainer for me because nothing stands in the way of me and a big Christmas tree in my living room.

Considering the space (or spaces) where you put your tree (or trees) will be occupied, it's a good time to sweep, clean, and ready the areas. Since I have a live tree in my living room, I also place a large industrial garbage bag on the floor where the tree will go. I nestle it in the open position. This is all to

ensure I don't damage my rug or floor if water from the tree leaks. It also creates a platform for me to set the tree when I remove it from the base at the end of the season (this, too, acts as a barrier from sap and water, which can be damaging to surfaces). This same scenario works for tabletop trees as well.

I also bring the base, lights, and ornaments from storage and do some preliminary setup before the decorating begins. Most importantly, I test lights to make sure they work, have extension cords ready, and make sure I've located the hangers for the ornaments. Hunting for these items after the decorating begins can be a real buzzkill!

Of course there's that old saying about the best laid plans . . . I always plan to decorate my trees the first Friday in December, but some years I get excited and start earlier. That said, I reserve Thursday night for bringing in the live tree. If there's rain, I wait until Friday. Then the decorating begins—and it usually continues until December 25!

Live trees waiting to be brought home and decorated.

## LIVE OR ARTIFICIAL

I've had live trees and I've had artificial trees and now I've got both. For me, nothing beats the look, feel, and smell of a live tree in my home, but it is a lot more work than artificial, so I completely understand why people opt for them. In fact I prefer them for tabletop trees and have several of them. The live tree, however, is the biggest and most prominent.

While there are a myriad lovely live options, I always go with a Balsam Fir. I find they have the strongest branches, are very hearty, and can hold the most ornaments. Each year I go to the same tree vendors and enjoy the whole process of sizing up and selecting the right tree. I always ask for a fresh cut. Right after they do that, I have them put the base on. (I always bring it along.) I find that having them do this while the tree is lying on its side gets it on straight and snug.

When I get the tree home, I set it up, water it immediately, and let it begin to settle. I always use warm water and add a bit of sugar. I try to let the tree settle overnight, as it often doubles in width and fullness. It's fun to wake in the morning and see just how full it's become . . . and to enjoy the wonderful fragrance. Important: I also check the water level, as it is not uncommon for a large tree to soak up an entire base full of water on its first night in its new home.

Since no live tree is perfectly formed, I often take time the morning after its arrived to trim any stray branches with pruning shears. I also often remove several branches along the bottom because the weight of ornaments can drag down branches, so I like to ensure there's a nice amount of room under the tree for the décor that goes there—along with the presents! I save the branches and often use them in vases, to which I sometimes add red roses or cut poinsettias (see the following chapter for more ideas). I also frequently use the greens on the mantle, bookshelves, side tables, and other areas of my home.

## MAKE IT GLOW

Before any ornaments go on the tree, it needs to be lit. While many simply wrap the lights around the tree in a downward spiral, I've found that this method doesn't do the best job of illuminating silvered glass ornaments. Through a number of years in trial and effort mode, I found that starting at the top and weaving the lights in and out of the branches provides the best glow and illumination of ornaments.

As I mentioned in the lighting chapter, I use new, clear miniature white lights. They generally come in sets of 250, and I use about 10 sets, which winds up being about 2,500 lights. Sometimes lighting the tree as tediously as I do can take a few hours, but it is absolutely worth it. Light sets plug into one another, but I also plug some into a green extension cord to avoid a short circuit. The lights and extension cord lead to a green power strip that I can turn on and off with the flick of a switch.

While in the process of lighting, I often take a step or two back and look for holes in the flow of lights and adjust them where I deem it to be necessary. Often after the lighting is done, I take some time to just enjoy the tree before beginning the next (and my most favorite) chapter: decorating it!

## DECORATING HISTORY AND TRADITION

In the earliest of decorating scenarios children were literally barred from the room, adults decorated the tree, and the children were under the impression that Santa and his elves did it the night before.

Since as long as I can remember, I was a part of decorating the main tree in our home as a child. I have many fond memories of just how magic it was to watch a tree come to life with lights and ornaments. But every family has its own traditions, both old and new, when it comes to tree trimming.

One tradition I love is that tree decorating often means it's the first day to eat Christmas cookies. It is hard work after all and I've got to keep my strength up!

## ANGEL OR STAR?

Growing up, my favorite TV show was *Family* with Sada Thompson and Kristy McNichol. I especially loved the Christmas episodes, where the it was the job of the youngest member of the family to create the star that went on top of the tree each year.

The first tree topper I made was an angel and I remember proudly placing her at the top of a tree filled with my other handmade ornaments.

Among holiday households, it seems there were almost as many who put angels on the top of their trees as there were ones who chose stars. Having said that, considering the number of stars out there in vintage venues, I think they may have been a bit more popular.

Since I do multiple trees, I have stars on some and angels on others. My favorite stars? An early German tinsel star, a large red and yellow American plastic star, and a silver Mylar Japanese star encrusted with red glass beads. As for angels, hands down, my favorite is a plastic American one made by Bradford. It is a silver angel, sitting on a cloud, inside a silvery semicircle. It is pretty heavenly (pun intended).

## MORE IS MORE

I've already described myself as a maximalist when it comes to decorating my trees, and this is where that aesthetic kicks into overdrive for me. Just as with the lights, I adorn the outsides and insides of

the branches with ornaments. While I abide by no hard or steadfast rules, I generally put the smaller ornaments up top and reserve the largest ornaments for the lower part of the tree. I find this offers a lot more balance and overall harmony.

Because live trees aren't perfectly uniform, I often fill in holes with smaller ornaments, and as I mentioned earlier, Christmas corsages once worn by my grandmother. Truth be told, my tree decorating continues for days and I continue to move things around for quite some time. For me it's half the fun and just part of the process.

## TINSEL, GARLANDS, ICICLES, POPCORN, AND CRANBERRY

After the ornaments are hung, usually the finishing touches of a tree include silver icicles or tinsel, multicolored metallic or beaded garland, or even strings of popcorn and cranberry. I've used all of the above at one time or another, and all have their virtues. The last option, popcorn and cranberry, can be fun on a tree with natural or handmade ornaments, while the rest of the options lend themselves more toward store-bought ornaments.

The truth is that as my decorating has evolved and increased, I've skipped this step to focus on maximizing my use of ornaments on my largest tree. That said, on smaller trees, I often use vintage beaded garlands that feel old-fashioned and are in keeping with the look of early feather trees.

## CHRISTMAS CONTROL FREAKS

I've gone in and out of having tree-trimming parties. While a lovely idea in theory, for Christmas control freaks like me, I often find others aren't quite as invested in the process and sometimes just randomly hang ornaments without regard for how the look or if they are size appropriate for that location.

If this sounds crazy, well, we've all got our idiosyncrasies and this is one of mine. The more I connect with other vintage Christmas fans, the more I know I'm not alone. So sometimes I gather a group of like-

minded people to help and sometimes I do it alone. No matter if it's a party of five or a party of one, moving the ornaments is par for the course. My loved ones have come to learn to not take it personally!

## A SKIRT BY ANY OTHER NAME

One of my favorite holiday sitcom moments is when the delightfully air-headed Bernice on *Designing Women* shows up wearing a Christmas tree skirt that Mary Jo gave her. Mary Jo takes one look at her and says: "Bernice, it's a Christmas tree skirt. You're supposed to put it around the base of your Christmas tree." Without missing a beat, Bernice replies, "Oh thank God. I like to darn never got this thing on."

Christmas tree skirts come in every size, color, and design. That said, I really just like to use green silk fabric

I had left over from a design project. I think it has a regal look and doesn't look too precious for its own good. I also like to billow the fabric around the base, making it look more relaxed than cone-shaped. For other trees, I've used old quilts that are also wonderful and not too fussy. Use your imagination and remember that doesn't mean having to spend a lot of money!

## TABLETOP TREES AND FEATHER TREES

I mentioned that each Christmas I decorate with both live and artificial trees. Aside from the big one in the living room, typically all of my other trees are artificial and pre-lit. This saves time and also creates a look I've come to appreciate.

I have some green versions, but my favorite tabletop trees are either flocked with "snow" or white. These frosty fakes beautifully showcase vintage ornaments and give a very welcoming glow. My favorites are made by Pottery Barn.

Most of these trees come in pots or even burlap bags. I don't love the way those things look, so I aggregate things like vintage ice buckets and even a mirrored wastebasket I found

at a flea market. I find they add to the vintage look and the shimmer. My favorite is an silver-plate Art Nouveau ice bucket. I don't even polish it, as the patina just adds to its charm. I also use mercury glass cachepots, also from Pottery Barn.

The earliest artificial trees were known as "feather trees" and were literally made from dyed green goose feathers. Authentic antique versions are out there, but they are often not in great condition. I have several newer versions made in the same style as their antique counterparts. The particularly nice things about feather trees are the space between their branches and their uniformity. As such, they hold a lot of ornaments and give a lot of bang for your buck. Originals were often adorned with candles, but I prefer to just use ornaments on mine and place them in illuminated areas like a mantle or tabletop where there is a nice amount of ambient candlelight.

## THEME TREES

For every taste, budget, interest, and color scheme, there is a tree. My trees tend to look more traditional with old mercury glass ornaments, but

I also enjoy doing a smaller WWII/patriotic tree.

In my early years of decorating, I also had many handmade ornaments I'd purchased at church bazaars. So I called it my "bazaar" tree. As my brother took it all in, he laughed and said, "Yes, it sure is bizarre!"

I've got other friends who do snowman trees, angel trees, nautical-themed trees, and trees with ornaments culled from their travels. The truth is that your tree is YOUR tree and doesn't have to look like anyone else's. The most important thing is that you enjoy it. So embrace your creativity and have fun!

## DECORATING BY COLOR

I know people who do all-pink trees with pink ornaments, lights, and decorations. Sometimes the actual artificial tree is pink as well. Underneath there's even a pink skirt. Others do green trees with blue ornaments and lights, etc. This monochromatic look really lends itself to Modern and Minimal décor. I certainly don't qualify in either of those arena. . . but when I see these trees in those environments, I think they look sensational .

The closest I've come to this look is all-white trees with silver ornaments, but mine still winds up looking more modern than classic.

## A TREE FOR EVERY ROOM

I am a big believer in having a tree in every room. So after the big tree is decorated in the living room (and sometimes even before), I start on the other rooms of the house. Christmas only comes once a year, so why not bring it into every aspect of your life?!

## FOYER

I have my grandmother's mahogany demi Lune table in my foyer and it's the perfect place for a small tree. I usually go for a tall, thin, white tree with white lights and silvery ornaments.

## DINING ROOM

Some years I place a tree on the buffet and other years I even place a small feather tree on the middle of the dining room table. As I mentioned, I don't light my feather trees, so with a taper candle on either side, it creates charming, luminescent centerpiece. It also catches the light of the chandelier overhead, so the ornaments really come to life. For this tree I use lots of multicolored mercury glass fruits and berries. I'm careful to use one that's not more that 12 inches high so guests can still see each other—and there's room for food and plates!

## FAMILY ROOM

As I mentioned earlier, bubble lights are one of my most favorite vintage Christmas creations. In addition to bubble lights on strings, there were also artificial tabletop trees made with bubble lights that adorned them. I brought mine with me to college and it was in my dorm room. Because they are smaller but provide a big impact, they can be fun and atmospheric. Note: these trees often yellowed and shed their artificial needles, so if you find one in good vintage condition, snap it up!

## THE BEDROOM

I like a serene tree in the bedroom and usually have another artificial tabletop tree with white lights. I don't use quite so many ornaments and often use paper and wire Victorian scrap ornaments or only pinecones or something that has a very calm vibe.

## NURSERY/LAUNDRY ROOM

Remember those ceramic Christmas trees that so many people used to have in their homes? Everyone I knew who had them placed them atop their console TV. Now they are out there in droves and are a nice option for a laundry room or even the nursery, since they are no fuss/no muss and even act as a night-light.

## CHILDREN'S ROOM

I'm a big believer in letting kids explore their own imaginations and experiment with what they like. For the vintage take on this, white paper cutout snowflakes and red and green paper chains are a sweet, easy look. Kids can make all the ornaments themselves, so perhaps suggest this idea and see where their creativity takes them!

## GUEST ROOM

If guests come to stay for the holidays, I love decorating their rooms. It is just another way to make them feel special and welcomed. Recently I had some loved ones come to stay and I surprised them with a small live tabletop tree that I decorated simply with white lights and simple glass balls. Under it I placed a 1950s light-up Santa. I made sure to make it easy to turn on and off and to not go crazy with size and scope so it also allowed them to easily navigate their space. As I did it, I felt as if I was channeling the kindness of my older brother when he surprised me as child with my very own tree, which he decorated for me. My guests were, indeed, surprised and happy. It's just a nice way to really roll out the holiday welcome mat!

## BATHROOM

I love vintage "bottlebrush" trees that were typically made in Japan and sold at Woolworths or another local Five and Dime store. They are often green, but sometimes pink and other colors. I like the ones that already have small red balls. I always use these in the bathroom, as they are ever so slightly kitschy and zero work to put up and take down.

Another great option for a bathroom is a tree I found recently that was designed like a triple-tiered green umbrella. On the tip of each wire insertion of the umbrella hangs a mercury glass ball. It was made in Japan and likely from the late 1950s/early 1960s. I'd never seen one before and had to have it. That's one golden rule of collecting vintage Christmas. . . there's always something around that you never knew

existed, and that's a big part of the fun. In addition, this tree is unexpected, fun, and unlike décor I have in other rooms.

## KITCHEN

The heart of the home deserves a tree too! Consider one of my favorite ideas: a small live or artificial tree in a mixing bowl. It can be adorned with something as simple as vintage cookie cutters tied with gingham ribbon. Or perhaps vintage children's toy kitchen utensils? Actual gingerbread cookies are also a fun adornment for kitchen trees.

Given the fact that the kitchen is command central, keep it simple. Placed on a sideboard or even in the center of an island, a kitchen tree is unexpected and always feels warm and welcoming.

The bubble light trees I suggested above for a family room are also fun in a kitchen. There's something about those bubbling lights that make me thing of pots boiling with yummy stovetop delights.

This "Honeymoon Express" wind-up toy by Marx was made in 1927. It has great graphics and sill works well. I like placing toys like this under or around the tree, where they may once have originally been gifted to children. Unlike electric trains, this toy is in one piece, so displaying it is easy.

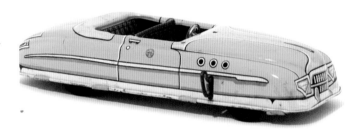

Like the Honeymoon Express train, this wind-up Marx car looks great under the tree. Its color and details are sensational. Hailing from the 1950s, this roadster convertible is a deluxe model. The Marx credo was "give the customer more toy for less money."

The late 1960s ushered in a mod look for just about everything from fashion to home décor. And Christmas decorations like this king and queen are perfect examples of that period. Larger in scale than many of their counter-parts, these two could be either hung on the tree or displayed on their own.

Candles like these three choirboys were made by the Gurley Novelty company were popular in the 1940s and 1950s. Seen as decorative, rather than utilitarian, they were rarely burned, and rather, displayed year after year. This trio belonged to my grandmother, who had them on her dining room buffet every year.

No matter the weather outside, it could always be snowy indoors, thanks to artificial snow like this, which was often used as a base to display holiday figures and ornaments. This 1930s box of "Christmas Snow" was never opened or used and it has great appeal on its own.

Gurley Novelty candles came in myriad shapes and sizes. This sleeping angel in a half moon and Santa are two favorites.

This quartet of German choirboys is made from composition and they are very light-weight. Typically displayed in a semicircle, they are a nod to Christmas church services and holiday hymns.

The December 1950 cover of *Family Circle* depicts two young girls decorating their tree. The girls are wearing homemade matching dresses, likely made by their mother. The tree is trimmed with a variety of blown-glass ornaments representing several decades of collecting. A homemade paper chain is also about to be added to the mix.

This spread in the December 1940 issue of *House and Garden* suggests "Yuletide Trimmings for the House." With a tagline that reads "Plumes and glitter, decoupage and stripes bring to the house a holiday tempo," this was a must-read for me. I often take inspiration from vintage publications like this. Perhaps next year I'll try the candy cane look for my front door . . .

Cardboard decorations like these reindeer were popular and inexpensive. The were often used as decorations at schools, club-houses, and offices, as well as in homes.

This center spread in the 1950 issue of *Family Circle* offers tips for readers on how to take the best holiday photos with color film.

This sweet cardboard Christmas tree hung on my mom's kitchen wall for years at Christmas time. I remember loving the large, round colorful balls.

These cardboard carolers provided an idealized holiday scene at a value price.

People used all sorts of things to hang ornaments to the tree—string, wire, yarn, etc. The first ornament hangers were flat metal pieces that could be wrapped around the ornament and the branch. They eventually were replaced with these hangers, which are similar to the ones we use today.

Old tin store signs like this one that reads, "Best Wishes for a BRIGHT XMAS," can be placed almost anywhere in the home.

# No Tree? No Problem.

## VINTAGE DÉCOR AROUND THE HOUSE

Not everyone has a Christmas tree, but that doesn't mean a home can't be filled with vintage holiday décor. In this chapter I'll give ideas for decorating for those who are challenged with time and space.

While I admit my trees are over-the-top (I make no apologies for this, since I think anything goes at the holidays), I think vintage décor can also be done in smaller ways.

Trees can be a lot of time and a lot of work, and I understand not everyone wants one. Also when there are small children around, vintage ornaments aren't always the best option for decorating a tree. If you don't have a tree or if you don't want to use your vintage ornaments on your tree, this chapter is for you.

While I add vintage touches all over my home, some people only want to do a bit of decorating in smaller ways. I believe this can be just as personal and impactful. My hope is that a few things in this chapter may inspire people who love vintage Christmas but don't want to do a ton a decorating.

For example, I have a dear friend who has her mother's glass ornaments, but she doesn't put up a tree. Each year, she puts them in a large glass bowl in her entryway, and they bring back good memories without having to create a lot of work for her. I love assembling beautiful old mercury glass ornaments in bowls and I often do it in many different rooms of the house.

Putting ornaments in bowls (glass, pottery, silver) can also be a different way to appreciate them, since they are not mixed with lights and evergreens. The ornaments alone are the focus and they can be appreciated for their patina, detail, and sentimental value.

## MIRROR MIRROR ON THE WALL

Mirrors in my home are always adorned at the holidays. I think of them literally as frames for all of the light and color and wonder that make up my holiday home. To add some interest, I often decorate them with strings of vintage beads onto which I hang vintage ornaments, which often have some special sentimental value or visual appeal.

On others, I drape boughs of greenery dressed with plaid bows and often other natural elements woven in, such as holly, berries, pinecones, etc.

I mentioned earlier that I tend to use new clear lights on my trees, but I still collect and decorate with vintage lights, and mirrors are one of the best places I know to display them. Whether figural or iced or multicolored, I find that vintage lights look great on mirrors because I can really focus on them. Also because vintage lights can burn hotter than their new counterparts, this helps me enjoy them without worrying as much about safety. I often wrap tinsel or artificial greenery around them and they look sensational.

## MANTLES ARE MADE FOR HOLIDAY ADORNMENT

One of the areas of my home to decorate is the mantle. Already a focal point in the room, a mantle is one of the most frequently decorated things in just about every home at the holidays. For mine, I enjoy bringing in greenery and placing it on top. Then I let my imagination take over. I already have electrified

candelabrum I purchased at the a Paris flea market, so usually add mercury glass balls to reflect that light. I also often fill vases with more greenery and add some other vintage pieces for interest. In front of the mantle I always have two potted poinsettias.

In the center I often place a wonderful pottery head of a sprite that feels very whimsical and sweet. Other years I add a pair of papier-mâché angels that probably once belonged to a nativity scene at a church. These are pieces that are in my home all year long, but take on extra significance at the holidays. Of course the final touch is the stockings, which I hang closer to Christmas Eve.

## BRING NATURE INSIDE

One of my favorite things to do at the holidays is bring the outside inside. Greenery, berries, pinecones, nuts, and fruit all make wonderful holiday décor.

Growing up in my house, I always remember my mother taking oranges and placing cloves in them. It's very old-fashioned and fragrant and sentimental. I follow her lead now in my own home and make a few of these and place them in bowls in the kitchen and the dining room. My only alteration is that instead of oranges I use clementines. I like the smaller scale and they are readily available at the holidays, so some get made into these wonderful fragrant orbs and some are in bowls in the kitchen without any cloves at all.

I also love to bring in cut holly and evergreen branches and arrange them in any and every vase in my home.

## CHRISTMAS ROSES AND OTHER CUT FLOWERS

I like always having freshly cut flowers in my home and the holidays are no different. They are, however, an opportunity to add a seasonal touch to cut flowers. I love red, red roses in jadite green vases with just a few sprigs of evergreen added to the mix. The same goes for white carnations and many other cut flowers that can be very inexpensive.

Some are surprised to learn that I also use poinsettias as cut flowers. Since they are plentifully available at the holidays in every grocery store, in addition to buying them to keep as plants, I buy a few extra and cut the flowers to add to arrangements. Red or white poinsettia flowers added to some greenery in a vase is a striking addition to just about any area of your home. By the way, as with most things, I didn't invent this. . . I take my cue from vintage magazines and other venues. This practice was quite popular in the 1920s and 1930s.

## A CHANDELIER TAKES ON EXTRA SHEEN

No surface is off limits when I'm decorating for the holidays. So sometimes when I run out of space, I have to remember to look up! Chandeliers adorned with boughs of greenery, bows, balls, or strings of mercury glass beads are all easy to pull off and pack a lot of bang for the buck.

Before I decorate it, I take my cue from the style of chandelier. For example, a brass Early American model would look great with greens and bows, whereas a crystal chandelier would do well with silver or red balls and strings of beads.

## DECORATING WITH DOMES

As I've mentioned, I shop with Christmas in mind all year long. Because I have so many ornaments and decorations, I'm always trying to think of new ways to display them. One way I've come up with is to use glass domes on wooden bases that I find at flea markets. I like to turn the dome upside down and fill with multicolored mercury glass balls. Then I put the base on and carefully turn the dome back over and place on a side table. I love the way they look and often recommend this to people who want to decorate with old ornaments, but may not have the time or room for a tree.

In addition, I've found any item or grouping of items placed under a dome take on a look of importance. If you have papier-mâché Santa figures, angels, snowmen, etc., consider putting them under domes. The glass of the domes reflects light in the room and items placed in them can feel like they went from ordinary to extraordinary.

# Frost the Windows

A very fun vintage touch can be had quite easily with a can of spray snow available at most craft and hardware stores. Vintage stencils are also readily available at flea markets and online auctions. Follow the directions on the stencils and you'll find yourself looking out over a frost-covered world, no matter what climate you call home. The stencils also look great on mirrors!

In addition, some tie vintage mercury glass balls by varying lengths of fishing line and place them in the windows. They catch the sun's light and give off more of a crisp, modern look.

## GET CRAFTY

I feel fortunate to have so many crafty memories of childhood. Some of the most special childhood art projects of my youth were shared with my family members. For example, once my grandmother and I made a large papier-mâché ball that hung from her dining room chandelier. I remember the experience more fondly than the end result, and that's why I love these projects.

She had me blow up a large balloon. Then we wrapped it with string we'd soaked in white paste. Once it was dry we, spray painted it, tied a bow on top, and voila. . . we had a very cool, crafty piece of Christmas décor.

I have other examples, but I mention this one because my grandmother was a busy businesswoman and her taking the time to do this with me meant the world. I also enjoyed seeing how her creative mind worked and appreciated that I was able to take part. Being a busy woman, she didn't always have a tree, but her home was always decorated with unique things we'd made or that she purchased over the years.

Many of my friends are busy working parents and by getting crafty with their children, they make memories and holiday décor. One family I know makes holiday mobiles with wire and construction paper and another makes origami birds and stars to hang from varying lengths of string on the rafters in the kitchen.

## HOLIDAY EPHEMERA

As I mentioned earlier, I'm a huge fan of vintage ephemera and use it all year long in decorating projects. At the holidays, however, I especially enjoy bringing out pieces that capture a moment in time and offer true glimpses into Christmases past. Such is the case with a Coca-Cola poster I place on the back of a door each year. It features a very jolly Santa enjoying a Coke and a Christmas feast brought to him by his elves. It's probably from the early 1960s and is just wonderful in every way. It's got great artwork, great color and fun subject matter. People love it because they have their own memories of seeing it or similar versions when they were growing up.

Another favorite ephemeral piece of mine is a 1917 WWI Norman Rockwell print entitled *They Remembered Me*. It features a soldier opening a care package addressed to him with the location "Somewhere in France." I purchased it framed in a well-worn black frame and I replace a piece of artwork with this framed print each holiday season. This is another tip for the space-challenged: Frame holiday ephemeral finds like this and swap them out for something that normally hangs in your home the rest of the year. I also do this with a number of early 1900s hand-painted French greeting cards I've framed.

## USE OLD THINGS IN NEW WAYS

I have three choirboy candles that were always on my grandmother's buffet in her dining room. When she gave them to me, she recalled that she purchased them at Woolworth's in my

hometown. She told me that she didn't have much money that Christmas so they were the only decorations she bought that year. They were special to her, so now they are special to me, and each year when I bring them out, I think of her.

That said, my current dining room is too small for a buffet so the choirboys now spend the holidays on a shelf in the bathroom. I see them all the time and they make me smile. Part of decorating with vintage and inherited items often means switching things up when you use them today and this is one of many examples I have in my own repertoire.

Along these same lines, I often aggregate everyday vintage objects such as silver items that run the gamut from candlesticks to mercury glass vases to framed mirrors. I like to group them together and add some silver ornaments, candles, and greens to the mix for a very chic table scape.

Also, I've discussed how I like to use old holiday gift boxes under the tree and in other areas. If you don't have a tree, they can look wonderful stacked on bookshelves, in baskets, or on side tables. And since it can be challenging to make room for holiday

décor if you live in a small space, use the boxes to hide items that you need to remove to make room for what you're bringing in. Believe me, years of living in New York City have taught me to cheat on finding space for things!

## ELF ON THE SHELF . . . AND THE BOOKCASE AND THE LAMPSHADE . . .

As far as I can tell the "Elf on the Shelf" craze is relatively new, with the book and the fun around it all emerging in 2004. I love that there's a fun, new tradition for kids and parents to share together. But I'm here to tell you that elves have been sitting on shelves for many, many years. Generally known as "huggers," vintage felt elves with plastic heads were very popular in mid-century American homes. Their name derives from their seated position with their arms wrapped around their knees. While often adorning trees, huggers also can be placed all over the house or grouped in areas—including shelves.

Other elves are made from rubber and are shaped in a way that enables them to grab onto the edges of many surfaces. When I was growing up, my Mom always had one on our telephone in the kitchen. I now have that one and have him perched on a lampshade.

Still more elves were made in ceramic in mostly red and green color combinations. Nestle them in potted plants, place them on the coffee table or move them around a la "Elf on the Shelf." However you decide to use them, these impish fellows are an awful lot of fun.

## BOTTLE BRUSH TREES AND CARDBOARD HOUSES

I mentioned in the last chapter that I use a larger bottlebrush tree in the bathroom, but smaller versions are even more common. Made in Japan, bottlebrush trees are common finds at flea markets and other vintage venues. Typically green and often flocked with a bit of "snow," these sweet little trees are usually in red wooden bases. They also come in red, pink, and other colors. I like the way they look grouped together, adding a sweet vintage touch to just about anywhere in your home.

Also made in Japan, cardboard houses are very common vintage finds and are typically in pastel colors with Mylar windows—and adorned with glitter and "snow." Originally intended to have a light bulb inserted in the back, I also now like assembling them in groups, sometimes atop glittered cotton batting (found in just about any drugstore seasonal isle) and enjoying them in their sweet vintage simplicity. With an array of offerings that includes homes, churches, stores, etc., you may start a village of

your own. And while you're at it, why not pepper in some of those bottle-brush trees for the sweet look of a vintage-y winter wonderland.

## LINENS

One easy vintage holiday touch to add to your home is to switch out the linens for something more in the spirit of the season. Vintage holiday tablecloths, runners, placemats, and other textiles are readily available in an enormous array of patterns and colors.

Often white cotton with silk-screened images of wreaths, holly, and other holiday images, a Christmas tablecloth was a staple in most American households, so they are out there in plentiful supply. If you prefer a new one, go with a solid red or green or a gingham combination of the two colors.

While you're at it, don't forget holiday patterned kitchen and hand towels. I have my grandmother's and they bring back so many good memories. I also have some new vintage-inspired versions and they do the trick as well.

Finally, back in the day, every hostess wore an apron, and there are many adorable vintage holiday aprons on the market. So if you're feeling like wearing a little vintage holiday textile, seek out one of these. I guarantee you that you'll get compliments from your guests. When not wearing it, a holiday apron hung in the kitchen is always a nice, homey vintage touch.

## SWEET SURPRISES

Christmas and candy go hand in hand. Of course the quintessential holiday confection is the trusty candy cane, which reportedly dates back to the late 1600s, when a choirmaster wanted give children something to keep them quiet in church. He requested a candy stick in the shape of a cane to remind the children of the shepherds that followed the Star of Bethlehem.

Since their early ecclesiastical roots, candy canes have come a long way to represent the child in all of us at Christmastime. Each year I buy boxes of them and use them around the house in festive vignettes. I particular like them in bowls or hung around the perimeter of vases.

Use old champagne glasses as candy dishes—especially if you don't have a whole set!

Another confection that feels very festive by design is known as "ribbon candy" and comes in myriad color combinations. Made literally to resemble ribbon, it is lovely and has a decidedly vintage vibe. Colorful foil-wrapped candies also look great when displayed in a thoughtful way.

Consider placing one of each type of candy in clear-glass, lidded jars in varying sizes. Since I like displaying things in threes, I usually have a jar of each of the abovementioned candies on a silver tray

A word of caution: These candies have a way of disappearing quickly, so keep backup candy in secret hiding places to replenish your display. I know in my house these lidded jars are in a constant state of flux, but it's all part of the fun. That said, placing them in lidded containers really does make grabbing one feel a little special—like being in a vintage candy shop.

## CANDLES GLOWING

Even the most minimal décor can include some candles, which always help to set the holiday mood. To get a truly vintage look, consider using glass hurricanes around the candles. A hurricane increases the glow factor and creates warm, ambient lighting. Add a few sprigs of greenery or holly around the outside of the hurricane, and you have a very vintage look.

I also love arranging candles on silver trays on the coffee table and other areas. To make it feel more vintage, just add some silver mercury glass ornaments to the mix.

## DON'T FORGET
## THE MISTLETOE!

Last, but certainly not least, Christmas is a time to get some kissing action going! Sprigs of mistletoe are available everywhere, so buy one and hang it in your entryway. For some a mere sprig is not enough, and they hang something known as "kissing ball," which is basically made of multiple sprigs of mistletoe.

Both live and artificial mistletoe and kissing balls are available, so there's no excuse not to add a little kissing bait to the mix. For a nice, romantic twist, why not add a sprig to a tray for breakfast in bed?

"CHRISTMAS is a season not only of rejoicing,
BUT OF REFLECTION."
—WINSTON CHURCHILL

A Victorian cut glass bowl with filigree work holds fruit eleven months of the year, but in December, it, and many other bowls in my home hold ornaments. Like the dome displays, bowls filled with ornaments are also a nice option for those who don't put up a tree.

This porcelain bowl with bronze accents is typically in my dining room or on the mantle in the living room. I usually fill it with oranges or greens. At the holidays, it's filled with ornaments that catch the light and look very festive. For an extra whimsical touch, I added a 1970s rubber elf that used to go on my mom's wall mount phone in the kitchen of my childhood home.

A clear leaded glass candy bowl filled with vintage silver and white ornaments takes on a decidedly wintery glow. I often place bowls like this on bookshelves or sideboards. If you have small children around and don't want to use glass ornaments on your tree, this is another way to display them, as long as they are out of reach. I also like these displayed in the vicinity of my trees that use this color scheme. The lights in the room and on the tree reflect in these ornaments and they are showcased in a very different way.

Dime store Santa figures are in plentiful supply at flea markets and other vintage venues. This grouping of plastic versions offers but a small sampling of what's out there.

Domes are a great way to display just about anything. At the holidays I use domes like this, filled with colorful glass ornaments. Of course, I need to exercise caution taking them in and out, but once they are in place, they're not going anywhere. While I use these all over my home, in addition to my trees, this is also a nice idea for those who want a vintage touch without putting up a tree.

Japanese paper and cardboard houses are highly collectible and look great grouped together or alongside small bottlebrush trees, like the silver ones pictured here.

# Give a Vintage Gift

**W**hen it comes to gift giving, my friends and loved ones have come to expect that they'll receive something vintage from me. I've found wonderful gifts at flea markets, auctions, and estate sales. There's something for everyone on my gift list but the key is to shop all year long, because you never know when that perfect item is going to pop up.

A few of my suggestions for vintage gifts are costume jewelry, concert t-shirts, picture frames, artwork, scarves, vases, linens, books. . . the list goes on and on. Last Christmas, I gave a dear friend an early twentieth-century Italian charm with a cherub on it. She wears it every day and continues to thank me for it. Vintage gives often say very distinctly: "I saw this and thought of you." And we all know that when it comes right down to it, it really is the thought that counts!

Sometimes I take a vintage item and personalize it (like framing a piece of vintage sheet music from someone's favorite song, placing their business card in a beautiful vintage wallet or giving them a vintage wristwatch or piece of jewelry with their name engraved on it).

Other great vintage gift ideas include silver cigarette cases (I'll gift them as a business card holders; I just insert the card of the recipient or one of my own), vintage champagne buckets, and mirrored picture frames.

A 1950s photograph of boys in front of their Christmas tree.

Speaking of picture frames, one of my favorite things to do is to go to a friend's Facebook page and print out a photo of them or their kids or other loved ones and put it in a vintage frame. In this age of digital photography, people really appreciate getting a framed photo. And a lovely vintage frame really completes the package and makes a memorable, thoughtful gift.

Another variation on this ideas is to put special photos in small frames and affix ribbon to the hangers. These wonderful, personal ornaments are often the most prized as the years go on. In fact, I know many that have "family trees" with lots of these small framed memories.

Vintage gifts can be highly personal and sentimental, but some can be given to just about anyone. For example, I always keep vintage vases on hand, and when I need a hostess gift, I just fill one with store-bought flowers. It's better than bringing flowers that need a vase (not considerate to a busy host or hostess), and gives something unique and interesting that sticks around long after the flowers have died.

Flea markets and other vintage venues are filled with fun, interesting, unique items that have a soul and character. These are things that you don't find in retail stores, and they are unique, inexpensive, and a joy to discover. Another idea is to buy people something from their childhood (a favorite toy, a piece of their grandmother's china, etc. It can open a floodgate of good memories and really show that you put thought and love into the gift.

I recently did a television segment about the virtues of vintage gift giving. I brought in an array of examples, but the one that got the most attention from the cast and crew was the *Talking GI Joe* "Man of Action" doll with "Lifelike Hair." It is in its original box. Many guys on the set told me they either had him or wanted him when they were kids. So keep this in mind. Big boys love toys that were popular when they were little. I am certain the same thing goes for big girls!

For the budding chef on your list, consider buying a vintage cookbook. I love vintage cookbooks because they are generally uncomplicated and filled with great recipes that used fewer ingredients and pots and pans. Also you may unearth some long-forgotten concoctions that bring back fond memories of Christmases past. Most importantly, vintage recipes tend to have less fuss, less muss, and more flavor. You can have haute cuisine. . . I'll take vintage cuisine!

Recently I found a 1940s cookbook in Whitehall, Montana, and there's a recipe for tapioca pudding with peppermints added to the mix. All in all, it's about four ingredients, and I'm totally going to make it for a holiday treat. For more on that, see the upcoming chapter on entertaining the vintage way.

Books in general are also great vintage gifts. First editions of favorites as well as vintage holiday books are all great ideas. Some vintage books also offer a chuckle around changing styles and attitudes. Also consider a period decorating book for someone who recently purchased an older home.

This 1943 ad for Firestone Tires alluded to the stress of shopping and the limitations as a result of Wartime. While suggesting the shopper would save tires and gas, Firestone made their centers a one-stop shop, offering something for everyone on your list. I was delighted to seem several piece here that I own, including two sets of my china (Fiesta and Riviera).

Vintage cookbooks make wonderful gifts. They are fun, inexpensive, and often contain simple recipes. I also think it's cool to add a vintage cookbook to a larger gift, like a grill . . . or maybe even a trip to Paris!

And what's the best vintage gift of all? How about some vintage holiday ornaments or decorations? People are so touched and deeply appreciative when they receive vintage holiday décor that reminds them of Christmases past. Or sometimes it reminds them of the past they never had!

I once gave a box of vintage American glass ornaments to very dear Spanish couple. They didn't grow up with this kind of décor, and for them it is a special reminder of their time in the US.

Just be careful if you give a box of ornaments to a starry-eyed kid. You may get him started on a lifelong collection.

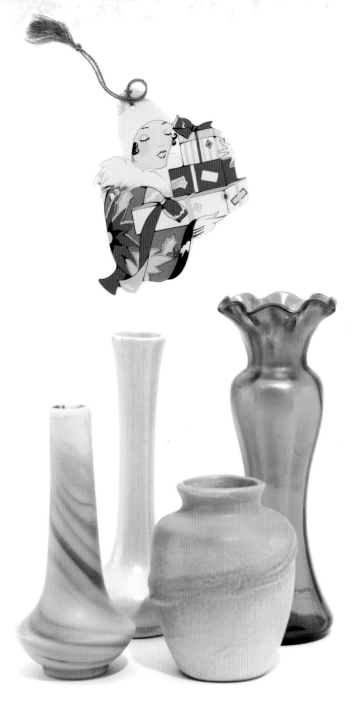

Once upon a time, bridge was a popular game for women's groups to play. I have several relatives who were members of clubs that met weekly or monthly, socialized, and played this game. This is a decorative Christmas Bridge tally card from the 1920s. The colors and image are wonderful. I find these make great ornaments and gift tags.

Flea markets have a plentiful supply of glass and art pottery vases like these. When filled with flowers from the grocery store or even from your own garden, they make a lovely and thoughtful hostess gift.

Individual letters from old signs make great gifts. I found this wooden "B" in Grapevine, Texas.

Vintage frames are in plentiful supply at flea markets, and they make excellent gifts—especially when paired with a vintage family photo. In this frame, I placed a photo of my Nana and Pop Pop, taken on New Year's Eve in the 1950s.

In this digital age, people appreciate receiving an actual printed photo. I like to frame mine in vintage frames I find at the flea market. This framed photo of my brother Johnny is a photo I gave myself last Christmas.

The cover of this December 1940 issue of *House and Garden* depicts many Santas flying through the stars as they deliver the most-desired home furnishings of the day.

A little girl gives her own money to a Salvation Army Santa on the sweet cover of this December 1931 issue of *Good Housekeeping*.

Toy catalogs is a great resource for collectors. Inside are not only toys, but also decorations and ornaments with detailed descriptions.

These are boxes from Hess's, my hometown department store. For a time, its brand icon was this genie that made everyone's wishes come true with gifts from this wonderful store.

Growing up, I thought my downtown Allentown, Pennsylvania, was a pretty magical place. We had three major department stores, and Hess's was the premier one. When I find vintage boxes from the store, I pick them up and often place them under my tree.

A very special vintage Christmas box from my hometown department store—Hess's. I like how Santa is busting out of the box. My friend and antiques dealer Janet found this one for me, and I couldn't have been more delighted.

Vintage Christmas boxes like these look great under the tree. I often give gifts in them and also use them to store decorations the other 11 months of the year. These were likely the boxes given to shoppers at department stores. I love that so many people saw them as special and held onto them.

I'm proudly sentimental and save a lot of little things with special significance to me. This little gift tag was on a present from my Grandmother, Carrie. She loved Christmas, she loved cardinals, and she loved me. I always tuck it in somewhere among my holiday décor and think of her. It's especially nice to open it up and see her handwriting inside.

I always say that a box of vintage ornaments makes a great gift. The one my dad gave me so many years ago started an epic journey of collecting that shows no signs of slowing down. My friends Tom and Josh gave these vintage Polish ornaments to me a few years ago. I love the bright, joyful colors and was very happy and grateful to receive them.

I was overjoyed when I found this rare set of WWII cardboard ornaments by the Merri-Lei Corporation in their original box. Representing both servicemen and their modes of transportation, along with the things they were fighting for back home, these decorations speak volumes about the patriotism in this country during the war years—especially at Christmastime.

# CHAPTER

## 9

# Cards, Wrapping, Tags,
## AND OTHER EPHEMERA

To truly achieve a very vintage Christmas, I don't stop at decorating. I also send vintage cards and use vintage wrapping paper, tags, and ribbon. Where do I find all of this? At flea markets—just like everything else!

Just like most every home had Christmas ornaments, they also had wrap and cards as well. Another item I often find are vintage Christmas gummed seals. I use all of these things and I find people enjoy receiving them, as they bring back fond memories of Christmases past.

These ephemeral finds are undoubtedly the least expensive and most unexpected of my finds. It's common to find unused wrap and cards for about one-tenth of the cost of their new counterparts, so in addition to being nostalgic and unique, it can also provide quite a savings! Have you looked at the cost of new cards, wrap, and the works? It's kinda outrageous!

## WRAP & TAGS

What looks great under a tree decorated with vintage ornaments? Gifts wrapped in vintage paper of course! I find that both rolls and sheets are in plentiful supply. Just like today, people bought extra when it was on sale and then it was tucked away in an attic or basement for decades.

These large mid-century gift tag stickers feature a sweet angel. They are great for adding a vintage touch, especially to big packages.

I love watching people's faces when they receive a gift wrapped in vintage paper. As with all of the other items in this book it can unlock a lot of fond memories. I sometimes take a cue from how gifts were wrapped in days gone by and cover the lid in paper, taping it to the inside. That way the lid can be lifted off and if the recipient wants to save the box—it's all part of the gift.

Ribbons and bows are a little less common, but they are out there. They often come in silver-wrapped packages that look like shoelaces. They tend to be thinner and more metallic than today's ribbon and also add a lovely touch to vintage wrapping. When the gifts are unwrapped, just make sure to save the paper and use it again next year. In addition to using on gifts, vintage ribbon looks great wrapped around a wreath.

## BOXES

I often find old Christmas boxes that once contained a gift. Often wrapped as I mentioned above, with the lid only covered with paper, these gems were often saved for fifty or even seventy years. Many people used them to store holiday ornaments, etc. I like to put them under the tree before the real packages are placed there. Sometimes I also use them to hold a special gift.

## CARDS

The first holiday cards were in postcard form and sometimes I find these and frame them (in a vintage frame of course!) for people on my gift list. They also look great arranged on the mantle or displayed in a bowl in the entryway (visual, interactive potpourri, I call them).

Like Christmas ornaments, I always gravitate to cards from the WWII era. I've got some in my collection that were sent from "Somewhere in Germany" and the notes inside say things like "Hopefully we'll be together next Christmas." Well, cue the symphony playing "I'll Be Home for Christmas" in my head. I love these tangible, personal piece of history and enjoy sharing them with friends and family.

Just as with wrap, whenever I see boxes of unused vintage holiday cards, I buy them. (Remember that off-season is best!) I particularly like the ones from the 1920s and 1930s as many of them have a decidedly Art Deco feel to them that is so evocative of that era.

Similarly I love cards from other eras because they really give a reminder of what the time was like in history. I've had luck finding lots from the 1950s, 1960s, and 1970s and recipients often call me and thank me for the memories they brought back to them. From the likes of Howdy Doody to Holly Hobbie, people love the nostalgia associated with vintage cards.

I've even found used cards (sentimental people like me saved them) and cut off the backs and attached them to new cards made to hold a photo. . . for an easy, memorable DIY vintage holiday greeting. (These photo cards can be found at any craft and stationary store and can even be ordered online).

## CHRISTMAS SEALS

Whether they were adorning envelopes or packages, Christmas Seals were enormously popular. Some were sold to benefit charities and others were just sold at local five and dime and drug stores. Large sheets of gummed seals can still be found for a nominal amount at just about any vintage venue. (Try online and many will come up). I always put them on the envelopes of my greeting cards for a special vintage touch even on the outside.

# Other Ephemeral Finds

By definition, ephemera are items that were not intended to last forever. Paper items like the cards and wrap are so precious to people because they not only bring back good memories, they are also rarely seen by people who don't spend time in antiques shops and other vintage venues.

This die-cut cardboard Santa decoration shows the Jolly Old Elf getting plumper, as he became more Americanized. He may or may not fit down that chimney!

The same goes for other vintage paper items. Just like with other vintage Christmas items, I am a big collector of seasonal ephemera.

## DIE CUT DECORATIONS

Heavy cardboard decorations were often used to decorate walls in school classrooms, stores, and even in homes. I know my mom always had a cardboard Santa and his reindeer on our kitchen wall every year. Many of these decorations were torn and discarded over the years, so finding them can be a lot of fun. They look great on doors, mirrors, and yes—in the kitchen!

## MAGAZINES

I love vintage magazines because they give an instant snapshot as to what a date in time looked like. What clothing was in fashion? What home furnishings were popular? What was happening in the news? What was playing at the movies? What products were popular? All of these questions and more are answered as you thumb through a vintage magazine.

I particularly love Christmas issues and buy them when I see them. It's fun to read the recipes, see how tables were set and look how homes were decorated for the holidays (many times I'll see ornaments and other décor that I've got in my own collection).

The ads are also as much fun as the editorial. I have a two-page advertising spread for gifts that could be redeemed with the purchase of Firestone Tires. As I looked around at the items, I saw my china (Riviera) and a number of other items I've got in my home. I also have a December 1946 magazine with an ad for *It's A Wonderful Life*, which was a real treat to find!

Similarly, vintage store catalogs are also fun to find and collect. While I naturally gravitate to ones from the 1920s to the 1950s to see the ornaments, lights, decorations, and other goodies, I recently found one from the 1970s that was a hoot to flip through. It is a fantastic time capsule and brings back a lot of memories, as do all of these things.

## PHOTOS

Like magazines, photos are literally snapshots of time. I always gravitate to photos of Christmas trees decorated with all the wonderful ornaments that I collect. I also love vintage holiday party photos and ones of people opening gifts.

Some of the BEST vintage photos, however, depict kids on a department store Santa's lap. I have a few that still retain the envelope they came in when picked up at the store. The envelopes are usually called "My Visit with Santa" or "My Trip to Toyland."

Like my idea for used vintage holiday cards, these, too, can be affixed to those photo cards I mentioned. In fact not only are they not just cards anymore, they are gifts—especially if you add a vintage frame to the mix.

## SHEET MUSIC

Whether it's "White Christmas" or "Rudolph The Red Nosed Reindeer," vintage holiday sheet music is fun to collect and frame. If you've got a piano, you can even play the songs. If not, you can at least sing them! I also had a friend use the inside pages (no graphic, only musical notes and words) of old Christmas songbooks to wrap her gifts one year!

I display this box as is—I love the sentimentality of it. Whomever these belonged to treasured them.

## ORIGINAL BOXES FROM ORNAMENTS, LIGHTS, AND DÉCOR

Perhaps the best ephemeral finds of all for collectors of vintage Christmas are the original boxes that ornaments, lights, and décor came in. Often adorned with wonderful artwork and graphics and great colors, these boxes look great displayed on their own.

Of course it's also nice to reunite them with the items in your collection that may have once been inside of them. That said, because old boxes can be fragile, I don't always store items inside of them—since I want them to be around for many generations to come.

MERRY CHRISTMAS ONE AND ALL
FAT AND THIN AND SHORT AND TALL
FROM
SANTY CLAUS

MERRY XMAS
HERE'S SOMETHING
FOR YOU FROM

I MADE IT
ALL FOR YOU
MYSELF
SO PUT IT UP
UPON A
SHELF
AND
DON'T
OPEN
UNTIL
CHRISTMAS

Grace Drayton (famous for her creation of 'The Campbell Soup Kids") designed these fun gift tags in the 1920s. With her signature impish faces and sweet details, Drayton made tags that would even make Scrooge smile (let alone "Santy Claus").

This 1931 candy box has great color and graphics. Just like gift boxes today, it was intended to be filled with special gifts for the recipient . . . in this case, a child. Most likely it once contained candy and perhaps a small toy.

Someone used all the Christmas cards but saved the box they came in. I like using these to store special ornaments and then I place them under the tree or as decoration around the house during the holidays.

This wee box contains its original seals. Interestingly enough, the sticker on the outside of the box reads "Merry Christmas," while all of the ones inside say "Merrie Christmas."

The classic font and style of this 1940s Christmas card is both simple and evocative of a distinctive moment in time.

These opulent hand-colored French Christmas Cards are from the 1920s. Their detail and vibrancy make them very desirable and frame-worthy.

With America in the height of WWII, this wonderful 1943 Christmas card offered some cheer. Important icons and slogans of the day are included, including Rosie The Riveter and a reminder to buy war bonds.

Vintage Christmas cards have wonderful graphics and sentiments. I pick them up all year long and use them to make my custom vintage greetings. They also make great décor for mirrors or other surfaces. Many are even frame-worthy.

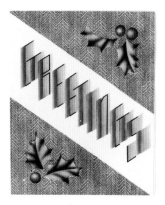

A hand-colored French Christmas card by famed illustrator Louis Icart. Given its beauty and rarity, this one merited a mat and a frame.

Hallmark continued to reinvent the Christmas card, as with this example of a 1950s box that featured works by "Outstanding Contemporary Artists." I think the box is as cool as the cards!

My annual holiday DIY project, I affix vintage cards I find a flea markets to new card stock (made to hold photographs). The card stock is readily available at stationary stores. People enjoy receiving them and I've even been told some of my creations have been framed. It's just one more way to add a special vintage touch to your holidays.

These fancy sheets of Christmas seals from 1936 feature the popular "Do Not Open Until Christmas" warning. When I use these to this day, people typically save the card or gift and open it on Christmas Day.

Some young boy or girl must've been very excited to receive this Flash Gordon greeting card in 1951. Made by King Features, this one's very collectable.

Like many vintage finds, sheet music is inexpensive and in plentiful supply. I like decorating with it and even framing some of it because the graphics are usually wonderful. Also, if you've got a friend with a piano, these make wonderful gifts. You can even invite yourself over for an old-fashioned sing-a-long.

"Xmas 1949." What a scene. I love this vintage photo I found. The kid's joyful expression says it all. I also love the family name on the drum. He must've been good that year, since it looks like he got Tiddlywinks, a fire truck, a tractor, a football, and lots more.

A 1940s die-cut cardboard Santa Claus with movable limbs and can either hang on the wall or be strung from the ceiling.

I often pick up vintage Christmas cards to use in my holiday projects, but it is rare to find an entire box of unused ones with their envelopes. These 1940s "Spang-l-ettes" are on die-cut card stock with foil backgrounds. Each has a hole for hanging, so the recipient could use the card as an ornament as well.

# Entertaining the Vintage Way

**H**olidays and entertaining are deeply intertwined. For many, annual Christmas parties and traditional gatherings define the season. Others look forward to certain recipes and entire meals that have become part of the fabric of their lives.

I used to have large holiday parties and each year I found that there were so many guests that I only really talked with a few. Now I like to have multiple smaller gatherings. I enjoy talking with my friends, eating some treats, and sharing my vintage holiday home.

It also seems that guests have a better time and are more engaged when there are fewer of them. We sit around the tree, listen to holiday music, and catch up. Since the groups are smaller, it feels more old-fashioned to me. Another plus is that people come together and seem to spend little to no time texting or making phone calls.

Of course entertaining for me not only means sharing good food—it also means it's a chance for me to use one of my many sets of vintage china and glassware. People enjoy drinking coffee from a cup and saucer and eating with silverware and good china. I find these items year round at flea markets and the holidays are a perfect time to share them with others.

I also enjoy bringing out family pieces that don't often see the light of day. For example, I've got my grandmother's champagne glasses and I fill them with foil-wrapped chocolates and other treats. It's fun to use them in a new way and in doing so, I also mitigate the risk of them getting broken.

In addition to dining, catching up and exchanging gifts, here are a few other ways I recommend entertaining your loved ones the vintage way:

## SING CHRISTMAS CAROLS

If you have a piano (or accordion or violin or harp) gather people around for a sing-a-long. Even the shyest of guests will enjoy joining in for a rousting versions of "Jingle Bells" and "Frosty The Snowman." And maybe wrap up with "Have Yourself A Merry Little Christmas." The nice thing about choral singing is that even those who may not have the best voices will feel comfortable and blend right in.

As technology has advanced, there's an entirely New way to sing carols. If you are the proud owner of a Karaoke machine, you may consider a Carol-o-ke-themed get together. People enjoy this modern spin on caroling, but I warn you that fights make break out over who gets to hold the microphone.

Of course the simplest way to start a Christmas carol sing-a-long is the old-fashioned way: a cappella. You can remind your guests that "Silent Night" literally started off that way. The newly written song was first performed in 1818 at a little church in Salzburg, Austria, where the organ was broken. So if it was good enough for them, it should be good enough for you!

## WATCH A CLASSIC HOLIDAY FILM

I love old movies and watch the same ones year after year at the holidays. For me, no Christmas would be complete without seeing George Bailey find Zuzu's petals

The most beloved Christmas film of all time, *It's A Wonderful Life* was produced and directed by Frank Capra and starred Jimmy Stewart and Donna Reed. This is one of the original ads for the movie as featured in the December issue of *Movie Show* magazine. Still immensely popular today, its messages are timeless, heartfelt, and universal. It is widely regarded as one of the greatest films ever made.

in his pocket. *It's a Wonderful Life*, reminds me of all that's important and unleashes a stream of happy tears.

Similarly, I love watching Barbara Stanwyck shine in my favorite holiday screwball comedy *Christmas in Connecticut*. She plays a Martha Stewart–type who really doesn't know how to cook or sew, but has to figure it all out for the holidays. Another Stanwyck holiday favorite is *Remember The Night*, where she plays a lady jewel thief whose heart melts at Christmastime.

My list of holiday favorites continues with Loretta Young and Cary Grant in *The Bishop's Wife*, and Robert Mitchum and Janet Leigh in *Holiday Affair*. Another fantastic one is *The Man Who Came to Dinner* with Monty Wooley, Ann Sheridan, and Bette Davis.

Of course no holiday season would be complete without *Miracle on 34th Street* with Maureen O'Hara, Natalie Wood, and John Payne. Edmund Gwenn did such an outstanding job of playing Santa that he took home the Oscar for it!

A newer classic, but a classic nonetheless is certainly *A Christmas Story* with Peter Billingsly as Ralphie who lives in a very vintage home decked out for the holidays. As much as I love the story, I also greatly enjoy the set and seeing all of the great vintage décor and home furnishings!

So while there is an endless supply of new Christmas movies on TV, I always gravitate to these old favorites. They really do bring me comfort and joy, year after year.

## WATCH FAVORITE CHILDHOOD CHRISTMAS SPECIALS

Whether or not there are kids at your party, bringing out classic holiday specials is always a crowd pleaser. Who doesn't have just a bit of sentimental attachment to *Rudolph The Red Nosed Reindeer* or *Frosty The Snowman*? My friends tend to really collectively enjoy *The Year Without a Santa Claus*. The

*Everyone Loves an ice breaker*

Ask your guests to share a story of their favorite childhood Christmas memory or their favorite childhood Christmas gift. It's a great way to keep the festivities feeling vintage and nostalgic.

best moment? When Heat Miser sings his song. If you don't remember it, and you were around in the 1970s, it's sure to come back to you once you hear it!

If there are kids at your party, oftentimes parents really enjoy showing them the specials from our childhood. It's sort of like passing the vintage torch and letting them become fully aware of your inner child.

## PLAY SOME VINTAGE VINYL

To set the mood, I love playing vintage vinyl at the holidays. I've got all of the old Christmas records that belonged to my relatives, or that I found at vintage venues. Remember those Firestone records they used to give away at gas stations? The ones with a whole host of artists? I sure do. And I have many of them.

As for the record player, I found mine at a yard sale in Pennsylvania for just $10.

Guests love picking out records, admiring the artwork on the album covers, and reminiscing about certain artists and songs. The experience brings back memories, often leads to lively stories, and fosters togetherness. Plus I don't care how many technological innovations there have been in the music world . . . I attest to the fact that music just sounds better on an actual record player . . . especially a wooden one like I was fortunate enough to find. The deep, resonant sound makes every note lush, warm, and very very vintage-y.

Now I realize not everyone has an old record player or records, so at the very least, consider cueing up a vintage playlist on Spotify. There are some songs that just sound better sung by original artists. "White Christmas," for example, has been covered by just about everyone. But I'll always choose Bing Crosby's version. There's a reason why it remains the biggest selling single of all time.

"My idea for CHRISTMAS,
whether old-fashioned or modern,
is very simple: LOVING OTHERS.
COME TO THINK OF IT,
WHY DO WE HAVE TO WAIT
UNTIL CHRISTMAS TO DO THAT?"

—BOB HOPE

I usually display this sheet music from one of my very favorite classic holiday films, *Christmas in Connecticut*, in an inexpensive frame near my front door. For other fans of this gem, this would also make a really fun gift.

---

In the wonderful *Christmas in Connecticut*, Barbara Stanwyck plays Elizabeth Lane (the Martha Stewart of her day), who has to come up with a husband, a baby, and a farm to host a soldier for the holidays—and she can't cook, so she has to figure that out too. Hilarity ensues, and it is a vintage holiday favorite. This lobby card advertised the movie when it was in theaters in 1945.

---

While not technically a Christmas movie, *Come to the Stable* does have holiday moments, and its heartfelt messages are sure to evoke a few tears and a lot of laughter. Loretta Young and Celeste Holm play nuns with unwavering faith who come to Bethlehem to build a children's hospital. Both actresses are wonderful in it and both were nominated for Academy Awards for their performances. Released in 1949, this is one of the original lobby cards.

Music is essential in a holiday home. And I still play vinyl. These compilation records from Firestone were customer giveaways . . . and most homes had copies! I like the graphics as much as I do the music.

The quintessential Christmas crooner, Bing Crosby, had many holiday hits, but "White Christmas" is the most popular and best known. This early set of holiday records by DECCA still sound great, and the cover always call out to be displayed on top of my pile of Christmas records.

This 1960 "Season's Best" record was a giveaway from Chevrolet dealers and features the very popular Dinah Shore, accompanied by Andre Previn.

# 11

# Storing and Preserving Your Vintage Holiday Finds

I prize my vintage holiday décor, and as such, I want to protect it for years to come. In this chapter I'll share storage tips and tricks for ornaments, lights, and decorations. Some will include how to ensure lights don't get tangled, ornaments don't get broken, and paper items don't get crushed.

When I first started storing ornaments as a kid, I'd pack them all up, and put them in the attic, but by July I had a hankering to see them, so I'd often bring them all downstairs, unpack them and take in their wonder. Ah the luxury of unstructured time in childhood! That is no longer the case, so when I pack my ornaments away each year, I'm literally saying farewell to them for another eleven months or so.

## PACKING ORNAMENTS

Because of the fragile nature of vintage ornaments, care in packing is really important. By nature, glass ornaments break and I've learned not to cry over broken ornaments. But if there's anything I can do to extend the life of my collection, I try my best. While not by any means a science, I've definitely got a system in place.

Inside my favorite storage boxes, I use shredded acid-free tissue, which helps ensure delicate old finishes aren't damaged. In addition, it cushions the ornaments and helps prevent breakage. Like the boxes, the tissue is made by the Ultimate Christmas Storage Company.

Storing my ornaments in between Christmases has become serious business. By far these are my favorite storage containers. Aptly named the "Ultimate Ornament Box," each one has two layers of adjustable compartments, is acid-free, and has vinyl zippered outer bags to prevent water or dust damage. In short, they are amazing.

## THE CADILLAC OF BOXES AND PACKING MATERIALS

By far my favorite ornament packing materials come from The Container Store. They sell large silk moray boxes in red and green with sectioned compartments for ornaments. So ideally, each ornament gets its own compartment. I've stretched this a bit with their wonderful packing material, shredded acid-free tissue. Why acid-free? So it doesn't hurt the finish of fragile old ornaments. (It's like hypoallergenic skincare products for your holiday treasures.)

I literally create "nests" of the tissue and nestle ornaments inside. Sometimes I am able to nestle several and the tissue ensures that ornaments won't collide and break. There are two layers in these boxes and they fit a great deal of ornaments. In addition, I often lay vintage greeting

Often when an ornament breaks, it is beyond repair. That said, sometimes, as with the case of this Victorian ice cream cone, it is possible. It takes a steady hand, some patience, and some super glue. You may not always be able to do it, but it's worth a try!

cards, cardboard decorations and Victorian scrap ornaments on top. After closing the lid, the one really ingenious thing about these boxes is that they include form-fitting plastic zippered bags that help keep the contents safe from moisture, dirt, critters, and a host of other potential problems that could arise in your storage area.

The price of these boxes and tissue is not inexpensive, but I consider it an investment. That said, there are many other avenues to keep your décor safe and dry.

## CARDBOARD, TISSUE, TINS, AND PLASTIC BINS

While not always effective at keeping out external elements, cardboard boxes with tissue paper are always an option for packing ornaments. Only use white tissue, as colored tissue and newspaper can actually transfer ink to your ornaments and potentially cause irreversible damage.

I still use a number of plastic bins for decorations and ornaments that are still in their original boxes. I do a little padding with tissue paper to mitigate risk of breakage. Time saving tip: Consider clear plastic storage bins so you can see what's inside each one!

## WRITE A NOTE

Along the sentimental path, I'll also suggest adding notes to treasured holiday items so their provenance is known and so that future generations can enjoy them and understand their true value. My grandmother added notes to her boxes of Christmas items, often indicating when and where she bought them and any family significance. Now when I find ornaments with notes either written on the boxes or on pieces of paper inside of them, I find it very touching and a reminder that all of these items had value in people's lives before they came into mine.

Of course it is completely my personality to see sentimentality over practicality, so let me also just underscore that there's also reason to write notes indicating what's in each box. For those who are big collectors like me, simply

Christmas and fruitcake go hand in hand. While often the butt of jokes, fruitcake was enormously popular and often given as a gift in decorative tins like this one from Schrafft's. Today these tins are both collectable and useful. I keep my ornament hangers in this one.

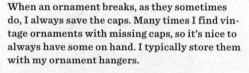

When an ornament breaks, as they sometimes do, I always save the caps. Many times I find vintage ornaments with missing caps, so it's nice to always have some on hand. I typically store them with my ornament hangers.

While I love my fancy ornament storage boxes, I also use smaller everyday cardboard boxes for some ornaments. This was a batch of ornaments from my friend Armand. He delivered them to me nestled in tissue paper, and I also store some this way.

writing "Xmas" or even "Xmas Ornaments" on the outside of a box isn't enough to avoid a bit of unpacking pandemonium.

I recommend getting specific when you label your boxes. Mine read things like "Ornaments for table-top tree in dining room" and "Garlands for mirrors." Taking a moment with a magic marker when you pack them up can help streamline the unpacking process the following year.

## STORAGE

Since many holiday items are fragile, extreme temperatures can be detrimental to their longevity. As such I recommend when possible to not store in areas that are apt to become extremely hot, cold, or damp. Unfortunately for most people, that excludes the attic and the basement, where holiday item are traditionally stored. That said, many of these items have survived the test of time and were stored in these areas, so like with all of the tips in this chapter, do your best, but don't obsess over it!

# Wear, Tear, and Repair

Just like with any vintage or antique items, pieces in your collection are subject to damage or ultimate breakage. That said, here are a few tips to help you keep your collection in good shape:

If a mercury glass ornament breaks, there is often little you can do, so learn to say goodbye and chalk it up to the cycle of life. That said, if the break is minor, you may be able to turn the broken part to the back. Also, if you have a steady hand and a little glue, you may just be able to make a repair. I still have some ornaments I repaired this way up to thirty years ago!

If a mercury glass ornament breaks, always save the metal cap and spring holder that keeps it in place. You are likely to find other ornaments that are missing caps and these will come in handy.

If ornaments are dusty, either blow the dust off or dust with a gentle piece of material. Do not use any kind of cleaning solution, as this may damage the ornament and result in a loss of finish.

## KEEPING LIGHTS UNTANGLED

One of the biggest holiday headaches is tangled lights. Anyone who's grappled with this knows exactly what I mean! I recommend taking lights off the tree and wrapping them around a large, heavy-duty cardboard tube. The Container Store also makes sensational rectangular plastic devices expressly for wrapping lights around them. They even have handles to make them easy to carry and manage.

## CONSIDER A TREE DE-TRIMMING PARTY!

There's something sad about taking down a Christmas tree. So why do it alone?! Everyone is so busy and overbooked at the holidays, but come January, schedules open up again. Why not seize the opportunity and invite some of your nearest and dearest over for a party to help you take down the tree?

What a great time to share holiday memories, catch up, make plans, and share New Year's Resolutions! By the time you're done gabbing the tree will be bare. And having extra sets of hands available to help take the tree out to the curb or to the recycling plant is always a nice thing. I have been that person who's wrestled a 10-foot, dried-out evergreen by myself, and I can honestly say that it's not fun!

From start to finish, decorating can be fun if you get creative and realize you don't have to go it alone!

# In Conclusion

## PAY IT FORWARD

You may have taken note that I mention my grandmothers often in this book. That's because they gave me many, many dear memories of Christmastime. Special meals, traditions, warm moments with family and friends—all of these special things happened in their homes.

I also mention my father and my mother who always made Christmas special. My dad, of course, gave me that first box of ornaments that started the wheels in motion for a life of collecting—eventually leading to me writing this book. My mom taught me how to make ornaments, and passed along old crafty traditions, like the wonderful orange and clove balls I make each year.

At the heart of it, this is what Christmas means to me. . . passing along warmth, memories, tradition, stories, and so much more. In addition to the wonderful intangible memories and stories that live on in me, they all gave me some of their own holiday décor to incorporate into my home.

So each one got to see their treasured holiday items take on new life in their lifetime. I encourage all of you to do this. Share your stories, traditions, memories, and your things. This lights the path for new collectors and ensures these things live on for future generations.

Especially in this culture of time-pressed, technology-obsessed, and often distracted people, I think it's more important than ever to pass along the things that really connect us. And Christmas does that.

So this Christmas I invite you to pass along something from your personal collection (an ornament, decoration, book, etc.) and include a bit of your personal history along with it. I guarantee it will make someone's day, just as the generous vintage gifts I was given have brought me so much happiness.

The older I get, the more I'm acutely aware that we really can't take it with us. In fact, the one thing I'm certain of is that the only thing we take with us when we take our last breath on this earth is whatever we gave away.

I spent a lot of time with boxes of ornaments that were tucked away in someone's attic or basement and are now being sold at auctions, house sales, etc. Little did their owners know the last time they packed them away, that it would actually be the last time they packed them away. The truth is, none of us ever know.

So give away something special this Christmas, light the way for new collectors, and keep the vintage holiday spirit alive and well!

MERRY CHRISTMAS!

# A LIST OF THE TOP US FLEA MARKETS
## AT WHICH TO FIND VINTAGE CHRISTMAS ITEMS

**Alameda, California**
alamedapointantiquesfaire.com

**Atlanta, Georgia**
lakewoodantiques.com

**Burlington, Kentucky**
burlingtonantiqueshow.com

**Brimfield, Massachusetts**
brimfieldshow.com

**Canton, Texas**
firstmondaycanton.com

**Chicago, Illinois**
randolphstreetmarket.com/
chicagoantiquemarket

**Lambertville, New Jersey**
gnflea.com

**New Milford, Connecticut**
etflea.com

**New York, New York**
annexmarkets.com/chelsea-flea-market

**Pasadena, California**
rosebowlstadium.com/events/
flea-market

**Philadelphia, Pennsylvania**
philafleamarkets.org

**Santa Fe, New Mexico**
santafeflea.com

**Seattle, Washington**
fremontmarket.com

**Springfield, Ohio**
springfieldantiqueshow.com

**Kutztown, Pennsylvania**
renningers.net

**Washington, DC**
thebigfleamarket.com/dc-show

# Index

Page numbers in *italics* indicate illustrations.

antique shops, 23–24

auctions, 26

bells, 46

birds, feeding, 106, 109

boxes
    about, *173–74*, 178, *183*
    from ornaments/lights/décor, *90–92*, 181
    for packing ornaments, 200–201

candles, *33*, *139*, 160

candoliers, 89

candy, 159–60

cards, 178–79, *184–87*, *188*

carols, 192

chandeliers, 150

Christmas Seals, 179, *187*

Christmas trees
    bottlebrush, *30, 31*, 133, 157, *162*
    decorating, 117–18, 122
    decorating by color, 129
    live *versus* artificial, 113–14
    parties, trimming/de-trimming, 122, 202–3
    room-specific, 129, 132–35
    skirts, 122–23
    stands, 53–54
    tabletop and feather, *30–31, 33*, 123–24

theme trees, 129
    tinsel, garlands, icicles, popcorn and cranberry, 122
    toppers, 118
    under the tree, 54, 56, *79*

color wheels, 85–86

cost of vintage items, 27

crafts, 150–51

die cut decorations, *141–42, 175*, 179–80

domes, 150, *163*

elves, *35*, 156–57

entertaining, 191–97

ephemera, holiday, 152–53

estate sales, 25

figures
    blow mold, 104
    lighted, 87
    wooden, 106

films, 192–93, 195, *196*

flea markets, 22–23, 207

flowers, 149

gifts, 165–75

history of Christmas decorating, 1–19

house décor, 145–63

houses, cardboard, 157, *162*

lights, 81–97
    blinking, 83, *93*
    bubble, 84–85, *92, 97*
    candle, 101
    clear, 86
    electric, first, 82, *90–91*
    figural, 83–84, *95–96*
    keeping untangled, 202
    reproductions, 89
    safety concerns, 89
    shapes, 86

linens, 158

luminaries, 101

magazines, *13–17, 140–41, 172*, 180

mantles, 147–49

mirrors, 147

mistletoe, 161

music
    playing, 195, *197*
    sheet, 181, *189, 196*

nature, bringing inside, 149

notes, 201–2

online shopping, 24–25

ornaments, 37–79
    American, 45
    beaded, 42–44, *66*
    in bowls, 145, 147, *162*
    earliest, 37–38, 40
    End of Day, 40

ephemeral, 49, 52

handmade, 44

hangers and tinsel, 42, *65, 70, 143*

"Keepsake," 53

lightweight, 40

packing, 199–202

plastic, 45–49

porcelain, 42, *59, 78*

reproductions, 56–57

outdoor décor, 99–109

paying it forward, 205–6

photos, vintage, *171,* 180, *189*

planning, 111–12

reflectors, 82

Santa Claus, *11, 18–19, 28,* 39

sleighs, 106

storage, 202

tags and wrap, 177–78, *182*

television specials, *78,* 195

vacation shopping, 26

wear and repair, 41, 203

windows, frosting, 151

wrap and tags, 177–78, *182*

**Ethan David Kent,** PHOTOGRAPHER
Days before Ethan began shooting *A Very Vintage Christmas*, he was trekking the mountains of Guatemala documenting the lives of coffee farmers. Before that he was shooting a CD cover for one of pop music's rising stars, before that corporate leaders on Park Avenue, and before that a nonprofit in the Bronx. Self-taught and self-motivated, Ethan brings a vision and technical ability to his work that sometimes defies logic. What began as a hobby is now his second dream come true. His first is living with his beautiful wife and charm-your-socks-off daughter in NYC. Learn more about his life and work at ethandavidkent.com

**Bob Richter's** passion for collecting holiday décor began as a boy. One day his father, who would take him to auctions, handed Bob a box of beautiful ornaments, including a blue jay, a Santa Claus, some bells, and other special figures, and said, "It's time you started collecting something and I know you like Christmas." So collect he did—and still does. That original box has grown into a collection that hovers at around 2,500 and counting.

Regularly featured in media outlets including the *New York Times, Entertainment Weekly, The Huffington Post, The Associated Press, Redbook,* the *Boston Globe,* FOX, CBS, ABC, and HGTV, Bob delights in sharing antiques, design, and bargaining advice. As "The Designer" and breakout star of the PBS series *Market Warriors,* Bob uses his personality and expertise to strike deals at flea markets all over the country and he remains a fan favorite. He also hosts *Flea Market Minute* and *Minute Makeover.* As a correspondent for *The Huffington Post,* he writes for the Home, Style, Travel, and Arts sections. He is also a Tastemaker for "Vintage and Market Finds" on the high-end shopping portal *One Kings Lane* where he curates special sales with art, antiques, and rescued objects. Specializing in a marriage of comfort and smart design, Bob offers up a fresh take on living with "stuff." His tongue-in-cheek mantra, "More is More," speaks to his love of art and antiques, which he culls from around the globe. As a contributor to PBS.org, Bob has profiled Pop Artist Peter Max, written about art pottery, WWII collecting, vintage Christmas décor, vintage clothing, and more. He has also served as Guest Editor of *NYC-Arts* and offers antiques advice in *eHow* and *The Intelligent Collector.*